THE CHINESE CONNECTION

CHINA

PACIFIC
OCEAN

Shanghai

East China
Sea

Taipei

Kwangchow

TAIWAN

BURMA

Hanoi

Hong Kong

Philippine Sea

LAOS

Vientiane

Rangoon

NORTH
VIETNAM

THAILAND

Bangkok

South China
Sea

Manila

GUAM

SOUTH
VIETNAM

PHILIPPINES

CAMBODIA

Phnom Penh

Saigon

MALAYSIA

BRUNEI

Kuala Lumpur

Singapore

Jakarta

INDONESIA

PAPUA
NEW GUINEA

Port Moresby

TIMOR

THE CHINESE CONNECTION

GETTING PLUGGED IN TO PACIFIC RIM
REAL ESTATE, TRADE, AND CAPITAL MARKETS

WITHDRAW

MICHAEL A. GOLDBERG

University of British Columbia Press

Vancouver

1985

THE CHINESE CONNECTION

Getting Plugged in to Pacific Rim Real Estate, Trade, and Capital Markets

©The University of British Columbia Press 1985

This book has been published with the
help of a grant from the Canada Council

Canadian Cataloguing in Publication Data

Goldberg, Michael A., 1941-
    The Chinese connection

Bibliography: p. 121
Includes index.
ISBN 0-7748-0222-7

1. Investments, Chiense - Pacific Area. 2. Real
estate investment - Pacific Area. 3. Pacific Area -
Commerce. 4. Capital movements - Pacific Area.
I. Title.
HD4538.G64 1985   332.6'7359'01823   C85-091215-6

INTERNATIONAL STANDARD BOOK NUMBER 0-7748-0222-7

Printed in Canada

To my friend and strong supporter
in this and related academic and
intellectual efforts . . .

David See Chai Lam

Contents

Preface

The "East" has long fascinated Europeans and North Americans. Initially, the fascination was based on ignorance and mystery surrounding this "exotic" part of the world. More recently, fascination with the region has taken a major upturn, this time based on emerging knowledge about the region's phenomenal economic development over the past two decades. The fabulous treasures of the Orient of centuries past are being realized today, increasingly through such mundane activities as trade and hard work both within the region and among its trading partners.

This study will be largely confined to Eastasia, a region which runs in a crescent shape from Japan and Korea at the northeastern point of the crescent, southeast along the China coast, past Taiwan, Hong Kong, The Philippines, and on to Singapore, Malaysia, Thailand, and Indonesia. However, at the outset, I merely want to indicate that the Eastasian region is already a powerful economic force and that by all indications it is likely to become more powerful. This is important background knowledge for the specific focus of this book, which examines the real estate investment behaviour of overseas Chinese, the vast majority of whom live in Eastasia. Thus, this book begins by looking at the explosion of economic activity in Eastasia (also called the Pacific Rim). This growth provides both the backdrop against which the overseas Chinese investors of Southeast Asia must be viewed and the source of much of the investment capital available to them.

Establishing the Pacific Rim context for this book is also important because it provides the proper policy setting for the concluding discussions about ways in which North American firms and individuals can become more closely tied to the region and to the network of overseas Chinese entrepreneurs so dominant there. Accordingly, Chapter 2 seeks to define the Pacific Rim region, to illustrate its scale, growth, and future growth potential, and to set the stage for the examination of the overseas Chinese in Southeast Asia as a distinct social, cultural, and economic group. Details of overseas Chinese communities and their associated commercial and cultural practices are dealt with in Chapter 3, which provides the other essential context for understanding overseas Chinese real estate investment behaviour. Given the Pacific Rim macro-context and the overseas Chinese cultural micro-context, it is possible to analyse overseas Chinese real estate investment behaviour directly, which is done in Chapter 4. Chapter 5 broadens the discussion by putting the overseas Chinese into the context of emerging international capital flows. Finally, Chapter 6 summarizes the findings of the book and extends them into the policy area to delineate a range of policies that could usefully be pursued to take better advantage of the enormous economic potential of the Pacific Rim region and of its most active ethnic/national group.

This field of study represents a new departure for me, and as a result I relied heavily on others to ensure that I was gathering relevant information and then to make sure that I was asking useful questions. Professor Terry G. McGee is primarily responsible for getting me involved in this venture. He obtained the research support to carry out the work and provided me with leads into the right body of literature. When it came time to write up my results, during a particularly hectic period of the academic year, he came to the rescue with encouragement. Several offshore colleagues were also of great help. Professor Maurie Daly, of the University of Sydney in Australia, a close friend of many years standing, by coincidence was working in a closely related field. He generously sent me copies of a book of his as well as several vitally useful working papers with current data and valuable references. I also want to thank Professor Nigel Thrift of the University of Wales, with whom I corresponded over several years. Professor Thrift's work was of enormous value because it placed my efforts in the context of the growing internationalization of decisions through multi-national firms and their behaviours and needs.

Dr. David Bond, a former colleague now a senior federal civil servant, was instrumental in getting me to move ahead with the policy portions. His insights on economic policy matters also served to keep me going in the right direction. Two people at U.B.C. Press were also extremely helpful, Jim Anderson, the Press Director, and Brian Scrivener, my editor, to whom I owe a special debt of gratitude.

Promises of anonymity prevent me from publicly acknowleging all those people in Vancouver, San Francisco, Hong Kong, Singapore, Kuala Lumpur, and Bangkok who provided me with access to their extraordinary knowledge of real estate markets and the world of business in the Pacific region. I do want to mention three people, however, who were instrumental in getting me these overseas contacts. First, Mr. John McLernon, president of Macaulay Nicholls Maitland International, a leading Vancouver-based Canadian international real estate services company, wrote endless letters and followed them up with numerous telexes to open doors for me so that I could speak with appropriate people. He also helped me organize my thoughts on the investment aspects of the study. The second person who made essential introductions for me was my good friend Mr. David C. Lam, formerly President of Canadian International Properties Ltd. As an overseas Chinese, he was able to give me the benefits of his knowledge of overseas Chinese culture and of Chinese culture too. A non-Chinese could not have a better and kinder tutor into Chinese ways. Third, Mr. Joseph S.K. Yu, vice-president of Manufacturers Hanover Trust in Hong Kong, formerly with the Bank of British Columbia, provided me both with contacts and a place to work.

Several other people deserve special recognition. First, Ms. Mabel Yee typed the several versions of this manuscript with patience, and she also tried to educate me in things Chinese. I also received extraordinary research assistance on this project from Ms. Cheryl Wong, who developed a superb annotated bibliography over two successive summers that provided the basis for the bibliographic materials at the end of the present book. She also dug long and hard for much of the data upon which Chapter 2 is based. Mr. Guy Young updated her table recently, and his conscientious digging also deserves mention.

Finally, as with all research coming out of the Faculty of Commerce and Business Administration at the University of British Columbia, our Word Processing Centre plays an essential role in revising manuscripts and in getting them into publishable form. They deserve more recognition than can be provided here.

One last set of acknowledgments is to the several agencies that helped to fund this work. The Max Bell Foundation of Toronto provided the bulk of the resources needed to conduct the research and to write up the results. The Center for International Business Studies here in the Faculty also provided monies to move the initial report toward publication. Finally, the Social Sciences and Humanities Research Council of Canada provided me with a Sabbatical Leave Fellowship for 1984/85 which gave me the support I needed to do the final rewriting. The Faculty of Commerce and the University also need to be credited for providing me with an outstanding physical and collegial environment for conducting this research.

In the end, despite the veritable army of helpers, remaining shortcomings must be acknowledged as my own.

1

Introducing the Issue and Its Context

As with most studies that in the end turn out to be broad in scope, this book grew out of local and specific circumstances. Beginning in the late 1960s, British Columbians became increasingly alarmed about foreign ownership of land. In the event, it was ownership of recreational land by Americans. Similar concerns quickly emerged across North America, spawning a diversity of controls and studies (Cutler, 1975; Horwood, 1976; McFadyen, 1976; and McFadyen and Hobart, 1977). Little empirical evidence was forthcoming to confirm the supposed widespread foreign ownership of Canadian real estate, nor was there evidence presented to document the harm assumed to accompany it.

These generalized North American fears of foreign ownership of real estate take on specific form in British Columbia, where they combine with longstanding xenophobia concerning Asians, particularly the Chinese and the Japanese (Adachi, 1976; Lee, 1976; and Ward, 1978), to produce undocumented and overblown claims about the extent of such ownership. Thus, bold headlines result when overseas Chinese acquire visible and important parcels of property, despite the much greater scale of foreign real estate investment in Canada by the British and Germans (Cutler, 1975).

The present study grew out of a general concern arising from the discriminatory attitudes directed toward people of Chinese ancestry and, more specifically and recently, misconceptions and exaggerations related to the increasing scale of real estate investment in the United States and Canada by overseas Chinese. Despite the intensity of feeling about the issue of overseas Chinese real estate investment and despite the duration of the issue (it began in earnest in the late 1960s at the time of the Hong Kong riots), relatively little analysis or serious research has been focussed on the subject. The objective of this book therefore is to shed light on this important international capital flow, not just in a North American setting, but on its broader Pacific Rim stage.

There are three areas where the present monograph seeks to contribute to knowledge and understanding. First, it is hoped that the findings concerning the investment behaviour of the overseas Chinese in Pacific Rim real estate markets add to day-to-day appreciation of the overseas Chinese as entrepreneurs and extend the growing body of literature on that subject. Second, the findings should also be of interest to scholars of entrepreneurial behaviour. Of particular relevance here is the very large pool of extant research which suggests that managers and entrepreneurs make their decisions with reference to an extremely broad array of criteria, many of which are completely non-economic in character (Simon, 1955; Cyert and March, 1963; Lindblom, 1959; and Etzioni, 1967). The present results support the notion that factors other than narrowly defined and rigorous economic and financial elements weigh heavily in the investment decision-making process of the overseas Chinese. Third, and finally, this volume seeks to add to public policy discussions by identifying a range of broader policy ideas that build on the specific findings of this study. These policies are intended to provide greater access to Pacific Rim trade and investment in general and to raise the level of consciousness about the importance of this region for the future.

Because the book has been written in a Canadian setting, it draws many of its trade and policy examples from Canada, but the discussion is considerably more general and is of equal relevance to business and public policymakers in the United States.

Attention below focusses on overseas Chinese real estate investment and its related capital flows around the cities of the Pacific Rim. Of particular interest are: why these flows take place; where they flow to and from; who makes these investments and how these investment decisions are made; and, finally, what types of real property are sought and how are they financed? The extraordinary growth of Southeast Asian economies has provided the basic fuel for these recent flows, and their anticipated growth is expected to provide continued and growing sources of investment capital in the foreseeable future (Chen, 1979; Geiger and Geiger, 1973; Hsia and Chan, 1982; and Hofheinz and Calder, 1982). Accordingly, the next chapter studies the remarkable economic performance of Pacific Rim economies over the past two decades, since these economies are the environment within which the overseas Chinese of Southeast Asia carry on their businesses and amass the capital base that enables them to invest in real estate.

In order to set the relevant real estate investment questions, and their answers, in a suitable framework, this overview is followed by a detailed discussion of overseas Chinese populations in Chapter 3. Of special concern is the history of the overseas Chinese and the distinctiveness of the overseas Chinese communities in the Pacific basin, most notably in Southeast Asia. An understanding of the "anthropology" and "sociology" of overseas Chinese business values and styles is also sought to provide the flavour of overseas Chinese business connections, culture, and decision-making. This backdrop is an essential introduction to the business sector of primary concern here, real estate investment.

An especially important element in this broad cultural context is the role of the family in Chinese societies, both in China and abroad. This role is not easily separated from the general business culture, but it is of interest in its own right. A final element to be explored is the role of land and property in Chinese society over the millennia. The strong ties to land and family are also not readily separable, but attempting to separate them does allow the initial demonstration of the unique place that land holds in the Chinese psyche and thus furthers an appreciation of the attraction that real property investment holds for the Chinese.

Having established the underpinnings of the analysis, the book proceeds to the study method and the geographical areas of interest. Data sources are presented and relevant related research is reviewed at the beginning of Chapter 4. The bulk of Chapter 4, however, is reserved for a discussion of the findings of the field research done for this study and their relation to existing literature on overseas Chinese real estate investment behaviour. An attempt is also made to connect the research results to the earlier discussion of overseas Chinese communities, values, and culture, particularly those elements dealing with land, family, and business activity. In Chapter 5 the discussion widens to examine emerging patterns of global capital flows and the networks that tie the origins and destinations of these flows together. A key concept is that of the global city where capital investment decisions are increasingly made.

The sixth and final chapter of the book begins by summarizing the argument and the findings. It then assesses critically the strength and generality of the results, a difficult task given the obvious absence of "objective" and "scientific" methods. Needed extensions to the present work are also raised in this last chapter. However, the major thrust is directed towards policy issues. Recently, a number of urban researchers have begun to observe the extraordinary connectedness of the world's major cities. It takes the form of a complex network of international capital markets that is evolving presently and that is built around several dozen key cities. This evolution of so-called "world cities" is of enormous importance, and it is presented in Chapter 5 to form the basis for much of the policy discussion that closes the book. Essentially, a flexible and innovative policy response is required to enable Canada to tap into the emerging world city network and into the dense network of overseas Chinese connections simultaneously.

2

The Pacific Rim Economic Milieu of Late:
The Go-Go Years Past, Present and Future

Since the overwhelming majority of overseas Chinese reside in Pacific Rim countries, particularly those of Southeast Asia, it is important that the dimensions of growth, trade, and population in this region be understood from the start. The strength of the Eastasian economic system has yielded the extraordinary opportunities for capital appreciation and accumulation of which the overseas Chinese of the area have taken such quick advantage. The contribution of the region's Chinese populations to this phenomenal growth must also be appreciated as Chapters 3 and 4 will show. For now, however, the macro-economic environment is the prime focus.

The Pacific Rim has attracted much attention of late, running the gamut from Japanese management techniques (Pascale and Athos, 1981; Ouchi, 1981; and Vogel, 1979), and the looming and awesome role of the regional giant, the People's Republic of China, to more general discussions of the remarkable economic growth of the region over the past two decades (Kirby, 1983; Hofheinz and Calder, 1982). What exactly is the Pacific Rim? Hofheinz and Calder focus on the eastern part of the region (thus their title *Eastasia Edge*) and include in their study Japan, Korea (both North and South), the People's Republic of China (hereinafter, simply China), Hong Kong, Taiwan, and Singapore. This limited definition zeroes in on the most rapidly growing components of the region. But it is too restrictive for present purposes since the overseas Chinese inhabit an area that comes closer to the notion of the Pacific Basin.

However, the Pacific Basin concept (Kirby, 1983) as generally put forward also includes those portions of Central and South America that border the Pacific, an area of limited interest here. Accordingly, a middle position is adopted, and attention rests on the Eastasian nations of the Hofheinz and Calder study, but also included are nations of Southeast Asia that they exclude, namely: Thailand, Indonesia, The Philippines, and Malaysia. Australia, the United States, and Canada also fall within this working definition of the Pacific Rim since all of these countries have significant Chinese connections and overseas Chinese populations. Central and South America are excluded as are the other nations of South Asia (India, Pakistan, Sri Lanka, Bangladesh, Burma, Laos, Cambodia, and Vietnam) both because they have few ethnic Chinese (Burma, Laos, and Cambodia being minor exceptions), and, more importantly, because they have not participated in the surge of economic growth that has characterized the principal economies that are of interest.

A look at the performance of the Pacific Rim economic system is now in order. Below are set out an array of data and tables that illustrate how strong and diversified this increasingly important region of the world is.

THE NATURE OF THE PACIFIC RIM ECONOMY AND CANADA'S LINKS WITH IT

The present section establishes the nature and dimensions of Pacific Rim economies. Of special interest are Canada's and British Columbia's trade links with these economies, although American economic ties with the region are also sketched out in considerable detail. The picture that emerges is of enormous growth with exceptional opportunity for Canada and, by extension, for British Columbia.

In beginning to review the data (Appendix Table 1), the scale of the region's population as well as its future growth becomes readily apparent. Particularly striking is the dominance of China, which alone represents between 22 and 23 per cent of the global population. Other large populations can be found in Indonesia and Japan. The size of the population in the region is extraordinary by Western standards and represents an enormous *potential* market, independent of its growth rate, which is also high, averaging close to 2 per cent per year.

Population growth, however, must be combined with disposable income to yield market potential, since it is the interaction of numbers of people and spending power per capita that jointly creates it. Such huge populations as those of India and Pakistan are excluded from the discussion here; they lack the requisite economic growth and purchasing power to represent significant potential trade opportunities for the intermediate future.

In addition, Pacific Rim economies are among the most rapidly growing in the world. Between 1960 and 1980 the gross domestic product of the countries of the region (with the sole exception of The Philippines) grew much more rapidly than did that of the United States (Appendix Table 2). Indeed, even such relatively developed nations as Australia and New Zealand had strong growth during these two decades, with most of the nations showing double digit rates. This result obtains even after adjusting for the massive population growth by putting output on a per capita basis (Appendix Table 3). The principal countries in the region all exhibit growth rates for gross national product per capita in excess of that of the United States. Compound growth rates in excess of 4 per cent per annum were recorded over the two decades by most of the nations in the region (compared with the 2.3 per cent growth rate of the United States).

Two other economic measures serve to illustrate the breadth of the growth of these countries. Growth rates of private consumption exceeded (in some cases by almost 200 per cent) the analogous rate of the United States, suggesting a strong market potential for consumption goods (Appendix Table 4), a potential that the region has met admirably from its own development, largely without foreign loans or subsidies. These countries also represent extraordinary opportunities for producers of both goods and technological know-how since their rates of growth of gross domestic investment have been spectacular by any standard, in some cases doubling their domestic capital stock every five years (as in Hong Kong, Indonesia, and South Korea) and every seven years (as in The Philippines and Malaysia).

Combining these data relating to population and economic growth leads to the conclusion that there are major opportunities for trade with the region. Large population bases and growing economies augur well for future trade links and capital flows, particularly when compared with similar data for the United States, which, while large in scale, is growing slowly and is highly competitive both from within and with other nations seeking to export into the U.S. market and to invest within U.S. borders. The region therefore represents a significant chance for North America to broaden its trading and capital base.

The rapid growth of exports and imports within the region itself is also important. For example, between 1976 and 1981, total exports to all countries from this region (note that Taiwan and the People's Republic of China are missing from these data) grew from US$124,148 million to US$287,173 million, equal to 131.3 per cent or 18.5 per cent per year (Appendix Table 5). Perhaps of even greater interest is the importing behaviour of these countries (Appendix Table 6). During this same five-year span, imports rose from US$122,583 million to US$293,150 million, or by 139.1 per cent, equivalent to an annual compound growth rate of 19.1 per cent, with growth in imports being distributed evenly across all countries. Another view of this trade is provided by ties within the Pacific Rim (Appendix Table 7), which demonstrate the dominance of regional trade. "Invisible" trade (for example, services) also exhibits phenomenal growth (Appendix Table 8). This is particularly important for the discussion later of world cities and financial services which are seen as key sectors of the future growth.

From these figures it is clear that these nations do present a great challenge. Canada has already been involved in trade with them to a modest extent. The pattern of Canada's exports and imports reveals this involvement and highlights the great potential that exists. Between 1979 and 1983, the most recent year for which data are available (Appendix Table 9), total exports to all nations grew from CDN$64,317 million to CDN$88,426 million, or by a full 37.5 per cent. During this same four year period, Canadian exports to the United States grew by 48.1 per cent, while trade with the People's Republic of China leaped by 165.7 per cent, that with Hong Kong by 60.7 per cent, and that with Taiwan by 228.9 per cent. Other nations such as Australia, New Zealand, South Korea, and Thailand also grew dramatically over the period. While four years is clearly too short a period from which to make any generalizations, it is indicative of the export opportunities. It also suggests that Canada is starting to take advantage of this potential.

Canada's imports, like its exports, paint a picture dominated by the United States (Appendix Table 10). However, here again dramatic growth in imports from Pacific Rim nations is apparent, particularly from Japan, Hong Kong, South Korea, and Taiwan, growth which in fact dwarfs that in imports from the U.S.

The foregoing give some indication of the magnitudes of trade and economic growth. They do not, however, provide any indication about the nature of the trade. A summary of the major commodities imported and exported by the Pacific Rim countries appears in Appendix Table 11. It is striking to see the extent to which Canada, a highly developed and wealthy nation, is dependent upon raw materials and semi-finished manufactured goods for its export trade compared with the manufacturing exports which are more typical of the growing and still developing nations of the region. This is matched on the import side, where Canada is an importer of manufactured goods. A more precise measure of these exports can be gleaned from British Columbia's exports, which represent Canada in microcosm and caricature form (Appendix Tables 12 and 13). Raw materials and semi-finished manufactures dominate the list with lumber and wood pulp the most important exports, followed by coal and then aluminum. Breaking down the exports by country of destination makes it obvious that Japan is the major recipient of B.C.'s exports and that these exports are all raw or semi-finished materials (Appendix Table 13).

While exports of goods have been considered up to this point, exports of services must also be reviewed. A particularly important export for Canada and British Columbia in the service sector is tourism, since it provides vital and diverse linkages with the Pacific Rim. Looking at both tourist arrivals and receipts for the years 1975 through 1980 inclusive reveals several trends (Appendix Table 14). First, Canada is an enormous tourist attraction, largely as a result of its proximity to the United States. Perhaps more important than the level of tourist arrivals in any one country is the rapid growth in tourist arrivals (Canada excepted). This implies a great deal of interaction with other nations, which is in fact borne out by data that explicitly provide a (partial) matrix of tourist interactions (Appendix Table 15). Unfortunately, data for such countries as Hong Kong and South Korea are missing, but the pattern is clear: linkages among nations of the region are large, and in view of the overall growth in tourism, these regional interactions are also growing rapidly. Again, there is a significant opportunity here, one that is obviously not yet realized.

The last few tables present a potpourri of data that yields some additional insights into communications within each of the countries and among them and the rest of the world. The pattern is entirely consistent with the explosion in invisible trade noted earlier (Appendix Table 8). The growth of foreign mail between 1974 and 1978 provides one measure of invisible trade. Canada's foreign mail is relatively stable, while places like Hong Kong and Korea have experienced considerable growth (Appendix Table 16). The pattern of foreign telegrams sent from each country is another measure. Most countries showed a dramatic decline, doubtless reflecting the growing use of such alternative communication media as telephones and telexes (Appendix Table 17).

That telephone traffic is likely replacing telegrams can be inferred from other information on the number of telephones in use and per 100 inhabitants between 1975 and 1980 (Appendix Table 18). Growth in this area is particularly impressive with phones in use growing by 36.1 per cent in Japan, by 62.1 per cent in Hong Kong, and by 120.8 per cent in Singapore during the five-year period. Finally, another indicator of internal communications and their improvements is given by the pattern of automobiles in use. Canada, Japan, Indonesia, Australia, and New Zealand have all experienced considerable growth in this area, while in Singapore and Thailand there has been stagnation in passenger vehicles, reflecting high duties and national policies to limit congestion and automobiles (Appendix Table 19). Commercial vehicles have exhibited steady growth in virtually all nations, which is consistent with the growth patterns seen in the economies of these nations.

The Pacific Rim region is, thus, one of the most rapidly growing areas in the world. Its rapid economic growth and large population base suggest a rapidly growing marketplace. The potential is great. Canada has already moved to take advantage of some of this potential. However, several points should be made about Canadian efforts. They have been limited with respect to the nations being sought out as trade partners, and they are even more limited with respect to the services, goods, and commodities being traded, a policy issue which occupies much of the conclusion of this book.

In summary, it is clear that, as Kirby observes:

> What is going forward is a global political shift, a new formation in international relations and an opening up of possibilities and linkages of the business plane of marketing, investment, development and modernisation on a scale not previously in view. It is vital that analysts and practitioners in all those fields, worldwide, who are not yet alert to what is going on and projected in the Pacific Basin, takes a direct and immediate interest in it. (1983, p. 97)

Focussing specifically on the Eastasia area (really the core of the Pacific Rim), Hofheinz and Calder epitomize the situation as follows:

> Seldom has the world seen such a remarkable pattern of sustained economic improvement. What makes it even more remarkable is that the improvement has occurred without many of the debilitating effects which normally take their toll on growing societies. The "growing pains" of development are remarkably lacking in Eastasia. (1982, p. 31)

Several authors have sought to get to the heart of Pacific Rim success and have provided intriguing suggestions about the causes of this economic phenomenon (Hofheinz and Calder, 1982; Hicks and Redding, 1982 and 1983; Wu and Wu, 1980; and Kirby, 1983). A unique role has been played by the overseas Chinese (Wu and Wu, 1980; and Wu, 1983), and the success of the regional economy cannot readily be divorced from the economic skills of the overseas Chinese communities. Nor is the growth of the region unrelated to the large capital sums accumulated by Southeast Asian Chinese. This interplay between the overseas Chinese in Southeast Asia, the growth of the region's economy, and the growing focus of economic activity in cities of the region (and in cities connected to these key cities) is of central concern here with the current focus on overseas Chinese investment in Pacific Rim urban property markets. Thus, the Pacific Rim economy fuels overseas Chinese investment capital, which in turn partially fuels regional growth, and so the cycle goes.

This background information on Pacific Rim growth and trade yields essential detail for the task at hand: the development of an understanding of one specific Pacific Rim international capital flow, that of overseas Chinese investment in real estate around the region. Armed with a broad feel for the regional economy, it is possible to discuss the more specific nature of overseas Chinese communities and their cultural values with respect to such diverse, but closely related, elements as business, family, education, and land.

3

The Backdrop: The Overseas Chinese, and the Role of Land, Business, and Family in Chinese Society

Given the macro-economic environment of the Pacific Rim region, particularly of the Eastasian portion of that region, it is immediately clear why capital flows of all kinds, including real estate investment flows, should have picked up so dramatically over the past decade. Hong Kong, with all of the uncertainty surrounding its future, right up through the signing of the Sino-British accord, is only a piece of the puzzle. Even without Hong Kong, the region and the overseas Chinese there are likely to form an enormous pool of investment capital. Essentially, Eastasia is booming, and the overseas Chinese have both boomed with it and been major contributors to its explosive economic development. Without understanding this macro-economic setting, the more micro social and economic foci of this chapter would lack the vital economic context within which these phenomena occur. However, it is necessary to narrow the focus of enquiry to look at the overseas Chinese in Southeast Asia specifically, including their social, economic, and cultural ties and behaviours.

Overseas Chinese communities have long attracted the attention of historians and China specialists (Purcell, 1965; FitzGerald, 1972; Williams, 1966). More recently, the focus has shifted to the sociology and anthropology of these communities and, in particular, to their commercial and cultural links (Wu, 1982, for Papua New Guinea; Chin, 1981, for Sarawak; Omohundro,

1981, for The Philippines; Skinner, 1960, for Thailand and Java; Olsen, 1972, and De Glopper, 1972, for Taiwan; Ward, 1972, and Silin, 1972, for Hong Kong; Ryan, 1961, for Java; Coppel, 1983, for Indonesia, The Philippines, and Malaysia; and Lau, 1974, for Singapore).

Clearly, there is no paucity of information about Nanyang (overseas) Chinese, which reflects the extent of their penetration into Southeast Asian societies. Attention focusses here on the Chinese of Southeast Asia alone because they represent the vast majority of ethnic Chinese outside China and because it is their investment behaviour that is being studied.[1]

Contacts between China and the rest of Southeast Asia have a very long history dating back to before the Han Dynasty (third century B.C.) (Purcell, 1965:8-22). However, it was not until the 1860s that emigration became of sufficient scale to be of concern to the Chinese Imperial administration. Also it was in 1860 that the Conventions of Peking (Purcell, 1965:29), at the insistence of Western powers, forced the Imperial government to allow Chinese nationals to emigrate.

Williams observes that the emigrating Chinese during the period 1860-1930 shared three characteristics. First, they were poor. Second, in common with most immigrants around the world at the time, they were motivated to move by hopes of improving their economic well-being. The third characteristic, however, differentiated the Chinese from other migrants.

> The Chinese looked homeward with enduring nostalgia. China was more than the old country. It was the only country worthy of respect and capable of being understood. The rest of the world was worse than alien. It was incomprehensible. Success abroad could be measured by the strength of a man's ties to China....This attitude of sojourner or transient was to become a handicap for Chinese abroad. (1966:40-41)

With few exceptions, emigration can be traced to southern China, particularly to Guangdong province and to southern portions of Fujien, Jiangxi, Hunan, and Guangxi provinces (Purcell, 1965:7; and Wu and Wu, 1980:122-31). Different areas of Southeast Asia received Chinese emigrants from different regions of China, so that in the Nanyang an enormous diversity can be found, reflecting the diversity of regions and villages from whence the emigrants flowed.

Some sense of this diversity, and the dominance in each of the nations of the Nanyang by people from one or two specific regions of China, can be obtained from Tables 1 and 2. Table 1 depicts the major language groups of the emigrants as well as the regions in China where those languages were spoken. Table 2 sets out the distribution by Southeast Asian country of Chinese regional dialects and shows the diversity that exists from country to country. It also demonstrates that in every country there is one dominant language group indicating a preponderance of immigrants into that country from a specific region in China. (Burma is a minor exception.) For example, Singapore is dominated by Hokkien speakers from southern Fujien, while in Thailand, the Chinese community overwhelmingly originated in northeastern Guangdong and are Teochius. Table 3 summarizes, as of 1974, the ethnic Chinese populations of the countries of Southeast Asia and shows that while significant in total (nearly 16 millions), they are a small proportion of the total population of Southeast Asian region.

TABLE 1
CHINESE SPEECH GROUPS IN SOUTHEAST ASIA

Speech Group	Percentage of Persons in Each Group	Areas of Origin in China
Hokkien (Fukien, Fukienese)	37	Southern and Eastern Fukien
Cantonese (Kwangtung)	24	Northern and Western Kwangtung
Hakka (Kechia, Khekka)	21	Eastern and Northwestern Kwangtung
Teochiu (Chaochow, Swatow)	15	Southeastern Kwangtung
Hainanese (Hailam, Hainanese)	3	Northern Hainan Island
Total	100	

Source: Wu and Wu, 1980:134.

TABLE 2
DISTRIBUTION OF CHINESE IN SOUTHEAST ASIA
BY COUNTRY AND SPEECH GROUP

	Hokkien	Cantonese	Teochiu	Hakka	Haianese	Other	Total
Thailand (1955)	7.0	7.0	56.0	16.0	12.0	2.0	100.0
Malaysia (1961)	31.7	21.7	12.1	21.8	5.3	7.4	100.0
Singapore (1963)	40.0	18.0	23.0	1.0	—	18.0	100.0
Indonesia (1930)	50.0	11.5	7.5	16.5	—	14.5	100.0
The Philippines (1965)	85.0	15.0	—	—	—	—	100.0
South Vietnam (1974)	7.0	60.0	20.0	6.0	7.0	—	100.0
Cambodia (1974)	6.5	15.0	60.0	4.5	9.0	5.0	100.0
Laos (1974)	—	15.0	70.0	—	10.0	5.0	100.0
Burma (1974)	25.0	25.0	—	—	—	50.0	100.0

Source: Wu and Wu, 1980:135.

TABLE 3
GEOGRAPHICAL DISTRIBUTION OF
ETHNIC CHINESE IN SOUTHEAST ASIA, 1974

Country	Chinese Residents (Thousands)	Total Population (Millions)	Percentage of Chinese in Population
Thailand	3,500.0	41.02	8.5
Peninsular Malaysia	3,687.0 (1975)	10.38	35.5
The Philippines	600.0	41.30	1.4
Indonesia	3,250.0	129.12	2.5
Singapore	1,579.9	2.22	72.0
North Vietnam	175.0	23.08	0.7
South Vietnam	200.0	20.40	0.9
Cambodia	425.0	7.89	5.3
Laos	60.7	3.26	1.8
Burma	500.0	29.52	1.7
Brunei	46.7	0.10	46.7
Portuguese Timor	9.5	0.61	1.5
Total	15,833.8	308.90	5.1

Source: Wu and Wu, 1980:133.

This historical mass movement of Chinese to locations in Southeast Asia can be attributed primarily to the opportunities that existed for them in the various countries. Williams sums up by noting (1966:10): "The Chinese settled, in other words, where they were tolerated and where their resources could be developed. They were attracted by the prospect of economic growth, and they stimulated development."

These economic opportunities drew the emigrating Chinese to the largest cities, such as Singapore, Jakarta, Bangkok, Manila, and Saigon, as well as to the rural areas where resources were being extracted on a large scale, such as the tin-mining regions of Malaysia. Flexibility and hard work allowed the overseas Chinese to prosper. This energy, economic success, and continuity of overseas Chinese peoples will be a recurring interest in this chapter. As with most of what follows, it is inextricably intertwined with the initial forces propelling Chinese emigration and with such institutions as the Chinese family and the Chinese family business.

The economic status of functions of Nanyang Chinese evolved quickly and naturally as they sought out economic junctures to service the colonial economies of Southeast Asia. As a rule, the overseas Chinese worked in jobs that were either foreign to the indigenous peoples or deemed to be below the status of Westerners and local nobility. They represented the first appearance of the middle class. While performing tasks in an array of industries and settings, the real contribution of the overseas Chinese to Southeast Asian economies was to the trading sector. In effect, they created the internal commercial ties of these economies and were involved in all sectors of trade from importing down to peddling in the most remote regions. In the process, they became intimately involved with retail and commercial credit, which formed, and continues to form as will be noted later, an important element in

Nanyang Chinese connections throughout the region. In this vein, Williams observes:

> It was inadequate to say, as did a much-worn cliché, that the Westerners held the Southeast Asian cow while the Chinese merely milked her. Before it could be milked, the cow had to be caught and brought in from pasture, and these tasks were Chinese too. (p.44)

By the end of the 1970s, overseas Chinese entrepreneurs had penetrated most sectors of the national economies where they were resident. The roots of Chinese economic activity in trade and industry are still apparent, as can be seen in Table 4.

TABLE 4
OCCUPATIONAL DISTRIBUTION OF ETHNIC CHINESE IN SOUTHEAST ASIA
(PERCENTAGES)

	Thailand (1955)	The Philippines (1954)	Malaysia (1970)	Indonesia (date unknown)
Government	0.02	—	—	0.6
Professions	1.59	40.0	—	1.5
Commerce and finance	50.84	41.0	24.0	36.6
Industry and handicraft	19.41	11.0	24.0	20.0
Domestic and other service	9.75	—	5.0	2.7
Agriculture	1.19	—	29.0	30.9
Unskilled	17.21	8.0	18.0	7.7
Total	100.0	100.0	100.0	100.0

Source: Wu and Wu, 1980:137.

Economic success was not without its contradictions: it resulted from the Chinese being forced into economic pursuits disdained by the indigenous peoples. This economic isolation further alienated the Chinese from host country peoples, providing additional pressure for economic success as well as discrimination and resentment. In short, economic well-being laid the foundation for the ongoing political difficulties which confront the Nanyang Chinese. These difficulties, in turn, gave them greater incentive to succeed economically and to remain essentially as visitors, hesitant to set down permanent roots for fear of persecution (Coppel, 1982: 3-8; Williams, 1966: 23-36).

The Chinese of Papua New Guinea typify the situation:

> The more the Chinese relied on wealth as their last resort, and the more they were involved in commercial ventures, the more envy or hostility they attracted, particularly after the date of self-government was decided . . .

After one hundred years of settlement, the Chinese in Papua New Guinea still share the same future of many overseas Chinese in Southeast Asia; that of utmost uncertainty. (Wu, 1982:162)

Few of the emigrants from China to Southeast Asia planned to remain. They viewed themselves as sojourners, resident outside China for a brief period of time to "make their fortunes" and then to return as wealthy and respected men, capable of maintaining their families through succeeding generations. This clearly put them in a double bind:

On the one side, the overseas Chinese, excepting some early immigrants in Thailand, avoided emotional investment in their foreign homelands and sought to divorce themselves from matters of local concern. On the other side, indigenous Southeast Asians concluded that the Chinese in their midst had come only to exploit. The Chinese affected detached superiority; the local people nursed resentment. (Williams, 1966:27)

Another way to view this dilemma is as follows: to maintain their culture is to incur the wrath of their neighbours; to yield to their neighbours is to lose the Chinese sense of community and also to lay themselves open to political and physical violence.

Education was instrumental not only in perpetuating overseas Chinese culture, but also in helping family enterprises to prosper. Education therefore was both valued for its own sake and for practical commercial purposes. An interesting example is provided by John Omohundro with respect to the Chinese of Iloilo, a small town in the Philippines:

Sons and daughters of the smallest petty merchant and the largest trader alike seek college educations. Filipinos and Chinese have attended college in enormous numbers in the last two decades. The most common specialization for Chinese is commerce, followed by engineering and business administration.

Sons return with these degrees to work for their fathers in the family stores. Fathers say it makes sons better businessmen who know more law and government, accounting, taxes, and economics. But status within the family does not readjust to the graduates because experience is held in greater esteem by the less-educated elders. A college-educated son is rarely, if ever, promoted above an elder brother with only a high school degree. (1981:147)

Literacy and education in their turn provide access to valuable commercial information, which further enhances Chinese economic status and calls forth additional resentment from indigenes. Education, therefore, plays a central role in the commercial and social relations of overseas Chinese communities (Williams, 1966:23; Chin, 1981:165-66; Solatt, 1982:164-65).

At several points so far, Chinese superiority in business has been noted. It is sufficiently important to warrant some separate discussion. Specifically, what are the unique characteristics of overseas Chinese business relations and styles (if any), and how might these be maintained, expanded and transmitted from one generation to the next?

Different authors have tended to stress different features of overseas Chinese business acumen, business organization, and business culture. One of the most interesting and important views about the basis of Chinese economic success in the Nanyang comes from Maurice Freedman (1979:23-26). Freedman considers a variety of facets of Chinese enterprises and concludes that the fundamental advantage possessed by Nanyang Chinese is their ability to handle money: "They accumulated wealth because, in comparison with the people among whom they came to live, they were highly sophisticated in the handling of money. At the outset they knew not only how to work themselves but also how to make their money work" (1979:23). This is of particular importance when considering the extensive network of overseas Chinese banks (both family and corporate) in Southeast Asia and the remarkable connections such banking ties provide. Since the flow of real estate investment capital around the Pacific Rim by overseas Chinese is of specific concern, the broader issue of the ability to move capital around the world is also of great interest. It will be seen later to mesh very closely with the emerging international economic order based on flows of information and capital among various "world cities" and capital/information markets (Cohen, 1981; McGee, 1984; Daly, 1984; and Kwok, 1983).

Overseas Chinese business in its broadest sense, including both relations within and among business units, is seen as possessing a number of unique characteristics. A great deal of recent attention has been focussed on the internal and external relations of Chinese enterprises. Hicks and Redding delineate a variety of characteristics which, taken together, can begin to differentiate Chinese business styles from those of other peoples. Speaking of "typical" business of the overseas Chinese, they observe:

It is perhaps most conveniently labelled as small-scale family business and, gathering together what insights may be had from a scattered and still rather thin empirical research literature, its principal characteristics may be tentatively proposed as follows:

1. Smallness of scale
2. Centralized decisionmaking with one key and dominant person

3. Strong family control via the occupancy of key positions
4. Low levels of structuring
5. A generally autocratic (though commonly benevolent) leadership style
6. A lack of formalism in planning, and high flexibility
7. Financial acumen of a high order
8. Reliance on trust in external business relationships (1983:5)

Family and kinship relationships, including a broadly defined extended family, are closely tied into business activities and are central to any understanding of overseas Chinese businesses and business cultures. Freedman suggests that family and kinship ties are so important because they are among the few over which an individual can exercise meaningful control. Business activities are above all interpersonal interactions. Accordingly, for the typical small-scale enterprise, family and kinship ties hold obvious benefits (Freedman, 1979:243), a point stressed throughout Lim and Gosling (1983) as well.

Several of the preceding points are worth elaborating. First is the degree of familism evident in the centralized control exercised by the dominant person (usually the father or eldest brother) and the reliance on family members holding key positions. Related to this is the generally modest scale of enterprises, which is consistent with great flexibility and informality. Evidence for this style can be had from various overseas communities. In Papua New Guinea, for instance, Wu found:[2]

Almost without exception, overseas Chinese societies demonstrate a common feature of entrepreneurship: the organization of kinship members in managing a small-scale enterprise which later expands both in terms of the number of kinsmen organized and the volume of business transacted. Business organization built on the basis of kinship has been characterized of commercial development among overseas Chinese living in both rural and urban areas, in developing and developed countries. (1982:88)

The highly centralized control by the dominant person recurs in studies of overseas Chinese firms. A specific example of this centralized control is provided by Omohundro for Iloilo businesses in The Philippines:

Chinese accounting methods symbolize this centrality of trust in the individual. The personality of the older uneducated immigrant businessmen, their inflexibility in a foreign culture, their reliance on kinsmen, and their simple management techniques all created commercial enterprises dependent upon single individuals. Managers and clerical staff are rare; such posts are indirectly filled by relatives. The owner is the bookkeeper, and the books are never available for examination. (1981:68-69)

Ward summarized this style of internal working relationships in the context of a small glass factory in Hong Kong:

Nevertheless, and making full allowance for the fact that smallness of scale anywhere allows a personalized flexibility in management and encourages acceptable paternalism, there remain some features to which, taken together, the phrase "Chinese way" can be meaningfully applied. They include beliefs about the value of education, the virtue of hard work, and the self-evident goal of economic self-betterment, shared by workers and management alike. (1972:384-85)

This impression of a unique Chinese approach to managing enterprises is reinforced when the internal organizational approach is set in the larger framework of external relationships, both with one's suppliers and with one's customers. A key element once again is trust, and it is manifest in a diversity of ways in the complex web of business and associated social relationships. De Glopper examined business ties in Lukang, Taiwan, and identified a number of aspects of business relations there that are of general and specific relevance in this discussion:

The very first thing to say about the structure of business relations in Lukang is that one does not do business with people one does not know. No one deals with strangers. Business relations are always, to some degree, personal relations. They need not be very close, but both participants in a business relation should be acquainted. (1972:303)

In such personal interactions, success results from far more than cleverness or sharp business practices. It is firmly rooted in the perceptions business associates hold of each other. The relevant concept here is that of *hsin-yung*:

Hsin-yung refers to an individual's or a firm's reputation, reliability, credit rating. It is the most important thing in business, a firm's most valuable asset. People say that to start a business one needs capital, but capital isn't enough. One must have *hsin-yung*, and to have *hsin-yung* one must know people, have a good reputation with some set of people, such as the other members of one's trade. (De Glopper, 1972:304)

Wholesale markets provide an excellent environment in which to study how reputation operates on a daily basis. Silin provides a specific example of how the concept of *hsin-yung* is applied in practice in the context of such a market, in this instance a Hong Kong wholesale food market.

> The importance of a good reputation was evident in all my interviews. When asked whether it was more important to be popular or to have a good reputation, one informant replied without hesitation, "A good reputation is more important. Without it you can't borrow and you can't get credit. You can't do business. Because of 'trust' we do not have to borrow from outsiders." (1972:338)

With so much emphasis placed on trust, it is not surprising that the informality noted by Hicks and Redding within Chinese organizations applies among them as well. Little in the way of formal contractual arrangements is made or apparently needed. Threats to one's reputation, along with community sanctions, appear to have been sufficient incentives to act honourably and to maintain good faith. Interestingly, though, as the Chinese become more assimilated, greater reliance on law and the courts seems to be emerging (Omohundro, 1981: 74-75).

Another unique aspect of Chinese business organization derives from its continuity and apparent stability over time. Perpetuation of the enterprise is an important and characteristic goal of all firms, but it is of special importance to the Chinese since the firm is so closely tied to the family and its continuance. The inculcation of business values in succeeding generations is a key means for achieving this continuity of the business and the family line. De Glopper cites a Lukang proverb on the subject: "It's difficult to raise a child who can do business" (1972:324). Indeed, if the family is to survive, so must the family business, and business skills must be taught at a very young age. Learning such skills is not independent of the wider educational process so valued by the overseas Chinese. In the current context, which links business, family, and commercial skills, the case of the Iliolo Chinese and the early education of children of Chinese shopkeepers is typical:

> As children, they learn to operate the adding machine and the abacus and to write the character script used in accounting. As they grow older, they are expected to fill any role that is needed, from janitor to sales clerk and cashier. They will accompany their father to Manila on purchasing trips and learn about credit and suppliers. As members of the family they will be expected to oversee employees, help at inventory time, load and unload stock, and so eventually participate directly in every aspect of shopkeeping. (Omohundro, 1981:146)

Business values begin early. For example, Chinese children in Taiwan from business families possess very different values with respect to business, profits, government, and competition (Olsen, 1972:292-294), confirming the anecdotal evidence from other sources (Omohundro, 1981; Freedman, 1979; Potter, 1968; and Wu, 1982).

Putting all of the foregoing discussion together leads to the conclusion that overseas Chinese business culture is unique in the region and a powerful economic force transcending national boundaries. Commercial ties among kin and associates span the Pacific Basin and beyond, providing a vital step toward economic integration and rationalization in the region. Indeed, Hofheinz and Calder posit that the sum total of these kinds of business relations has led to the creation of a sophisticated and far-reaching economic network binding the "Eastasia" region:

> Even before the great trading companies of Japan rose to prominence, Eastasia already possessed the beginnings of an integrated economic system. The extensive, business-oriented overseas Chinese community is still the background of much of Eastasian trade outside the trading companies. Though statistics are hard to find, it seems likely that the major share of trade among the five members of the Association of Southeast Asian Nations (ASEAN), including Singapore, is conducted through firms controlled by overseas ethnic Chinese. (1982:200)

THE FAMILY

One of the most striking features of Chinese societies to non-Chinese observers is the cohesion and importance of the family unit, both in its nuclear and extended forms. The institution of the family in China is a very old and central one. The family was seen as a key element in the Confucian order of a stable and harmonious state dating back roughly 2500 years. In microcosm, the family represented the whole set of paternalistic and patriarchal relations that ordered Chinese society. The individual had no place in such a social order, nor did initiative and personal freedom. Confucian society was based on an elaborate set of hierarchical obligations and submission to authority. The family was the fundamental building block.

> In the Confucian view, the family was the main pillar of society. Not only was it the smallest social unit in which relations of dominance-subservience obtained (although here somewhat tempered by kinship solidarity), and hence regarded as the very embodiment of the moral code, but it was

also, on the administrative level, the vector of the system of collective responsibility, for the whole family had to expiate for a crime committed by one of its members. (Balazs, 1964:155-56)

Family relationships were precisely specified in keeping with the need for hierarchy and order. Five relationships were envisioned which completely spanned all possible interactions among people. Above all sat the Emperor with his "mandate of Heaven." Then came hierarchically ordered relationships all the way down to those among friends. In his study of the Chinese family Baker sets these out in some detail:

1. Ruler/minister
2. Father/son
3. Elder brother/younger brother
4. Husband/wife
5. Friend/friend

Now these Five Human Relationships (*wu-lun*) were arranged in order of priority, and with the exception of the last one were all superior/inferior relationships too; and so they were intended to give guidance as to the correct weight to be put on any relationship. Properly observed there could be no conflict or friction within Chinese society or within the family group, for every member of the family and of society was held tightly in check by the duty and obedience which he owed to another (1979:11)

Trade-offs between responsibilities to oneself and to one's family are clearly weighted heavily in Chinese society toward the family and away from the individual. This is a dramatic contrast with the Western view in which individual rights and initiatives are seen as being of paramount importance. In some sense, Westerners view the family as a means to promote and foster individual growth and the pursuit of individual goals. In the Chinese family, this state of affairs was reversed:

It was not the family which existed in order to support the individual, but rather the individual who existed in order to continue the family. (Baker, 1979:26)

Within the family unit, there is a well-ordered set of relationships that parallel the five relationships noted above. These "three relationships" serve to mitigate disputes and reinforce authority within the family units much as the five relationships did at a societal level. The hierarchy to be followed within the family is: 1. Generation; 2. Age; 3. Sex. When combined with the five relationships, the three relationships imply that every person in classical Chinese Confucian society knew exactly his or her position. Everything was tightly ordered, "harmony" was maintained, and the "mandate of heaven" continued to be bestowed on such a society's rulers.

Father-son relationships are particularly crucial since they have enormous implications for family businesses and also for the smooth transition of the family, and the family business, from one generation to the next.

> Everything hangs on the relation between father and sons. This relation is overtly one of severe subordination of the sons and of correlative authority on the part of the father. In law a son cannot separate himself from the estate against parental wishes. (Freedman, 1979: 236)

Despite the apparent lack of ambiguity in father-son relationships, intrafamilial battles did rage, and brothers vied to succeed the father and supersede each other, though seniority still was of enormous importance in these fraternal alliances. Such vying, while counter to the prevailing Confucian ethic, was vitally necessary if the family unit was to endure over time because one of the clear weaknesses of the rigid specification of human and family relationships was its difficulty in allowing for succession. Junior members of the family were not given authority until the senior members passed from the scene. Intergenerational conflict and succession needed to be sorted out in some manner if the family and the society were to be perpetuated.

It is clear that while in any given period Chinese societal interactions were extremely well ordered, through time, it was much harder to keep things so well arranged. The passage of time and of generations was of enormous importance to Chinese society. In short, time was no mere abstraction. It was real and continuous, and the family held key responsibilities in knitting past and future into a continuum (Balazs, 1964: 108-9).

This notion of the family as the pivot between the past and the future provides further reason for stressing the family's role in society and rationale for subjugating the individual to the family's needs and will. The idea is captured in what Baker calls the "Continuum of Descent":

> By this I mean simply that Descent is a unity, a rope which began somewhere back in the remote past, and which stretches on to the infinite future. The rope at any one time may be thicker or thinner according to the number of strands (families) or fibres (male individuals) which exist, but so long as one fibre remains the rope is there. The fibres at any one point are not just fibres, they are the representatives of the rope as a whole. That is, the individual alive is the personification of all his forebears and of all his descendants yet unborn. He exists by virtue of

his ancestors, and his descendants exist only through him: and we shall see later that we can treat these statements vice versa with almost equal validity. To continue our crude analogy, the rope stretches from Infinity to Infinity passing over a razor which is the Present. If the rope is cut, both ends fall away from the middle and the rope is no more. If the man alive now dies without heir, the whole continuum of ancestors and unborn descendants dies with him. (Baker, 1979:26-27)

In all this striving for permanence and continuity in the face of change, land plays a special role. Shortly, land will be treated as a separate subject. At this point land needs to be seen in the context of the requirement to perpetuate the Chinese family and its associated kinship relations. As was noted at the outset, it is not easy to compartmentalize the examination of overseas Chinese culture, land, and the family. The link between land, and the family's continuance is an example of the interweaving of these subjects. Beattie, in fact, ties continuity of leading families in T'ung-ch'eng county of Anhui Province (eastern China) directly to their holdings of land. Land, therefore, becomes a central element in perpetuating the family and, by extension, the society.

There can be no doubt moreover that one major element in the survival of the enduring elite of T'ung-ch'eng ... was its continuous effort to secure its wealth in the form of land. All the great families of the county were built up in their early days on land. (1979:130)

Closely allied with land in continuing the family line is education. Earlier, education was seen as important for inculcating business values and skills and thus for extending the family, both over time and in wealth and influence at any point in time. In traditional China, education was to be pursued in its own right since it was the road to power and prestige. China's civil service, nearly two-and-a-half millenia old, was the first in the world to be filled through open competitive examination. To be a scholar was to have access to the civil service and the power and security that went with such posts in Imperial China. Land provided income and stability which allowed a student to study for the Imperial Examinations, passing which was essential for securing civil service posts. These posts in turn provided the wherewithal to purchase land and sustain the lineage. The land/education linkage carried on hand-in-hand over the generations, each being a means to perpetuate the family and kinship line (Beattie, 1979:126).

Land and education, therefore, are key elements in preserving the family lineage and keeping kinship relationships intact over time. In an urban setting, however, such as the ones in which most overseas Chinese find themselves today, land is replaced functionally by the family business as the means of maintaining the family. Moreover, until very recently in many countries of Southeast Asia, the overseas Chinese were prohibited from owning land (Wu and Wu, 1980; Coppel, 1982). However, unlike land which is viewed as permanent, business is riskier and more difficult to maintain over time. Omohundro cites a common saying among overseas Chinese in Iloilo, The Philippines, to the effect that "No third generation stays rich" (1981:145) or as they say in the Ottawa Valley, "shirt sleeves to shirt sleeves in three generations."

Thus, in a non-rural environment, business takes the place of land as the means of sustaining the family line. For the overseas Chinese, business becomes much more than making a living. Rather, it is tied to the perpetuation of the family and of Chinese family tradition. Thus, overseas Chinese business skill and success must be seen against the background of the family and all its importance, and not just as a means for achieving prestige and wealth in the short run. Chinese business relations are heavily oriented toward long-run relations and *hsun-yung* (trust), completely in keeping with the long-run view of the family and the need to keep its line functioning over many generations.

LAND

That business should supplant land as the basis for intergenerational stability is clearly a relatively recent phenomenon and one perfectly consistent with the situation of the Nanyang Chinese, which is overwhelmingly urban in character. Essentially, this substitution of business for land is a product of the last one hundred years. However, even in urban settings in the Nanyang, the Chinese have not lost their desire for real estate.

Land holds a central position in rural society generally. In a Chinese context this general importance takes on specific meaning, very much tied to the requirement of "Continuity of Descent."

> Throughout its history, China remained basically rural. The security of the family depended on the land it owned. To sell family land was like participating in a fraction of the family's death, and to buy land for the family was like holding a wedding, with its promise of fruitfulness and strength. (Scharfstein, 1974:5)

The evolution of the modern importance and conception of land in China can be traced to the end of the Chou period (third century B.C.) when land could first be held by an individual family head and by family units. (For a detailed discussion of the evolution of land ownership and property rights in China see Balazs, 1964:101-25.) In his classic history of China, Eberhard suggests:

> As long as the idea that all land belonged to the great clans of the Chou prevailed, sale of land was inconceivable; but when individual family heads acquired land or cultivated new land, they regarded it as their natural right to dispose of the land as they wished. From now on until the end of the medieval period, the family head as representative of the family could sell or buy land. However, the land belonged to the family and not to him as a person. (1962:54)

The land-lineage linkage is once again confirmed. In historic times land and kinship were inextricably linked. The pull of the land, however, even today, and even among Chinese people who have never visited their ancestral villages, is extremely strong and meaningful.

> Land, constant in space and time, was the "anchor against the wind" which gave permanence to the kinship group even while its members came and went over generations. Chinese people still ask each other "Where is your native land?" as a matter of importance to mutual understanding. In many cases the answer which is given may appear false in that the person concerned may never have been there in his life, but is the place from which his father or even grandfather came, the place of his ancestral lands, and even if he no longer has a direct claim on those lands he has a deeply felt loyalty to them. (Baker, 1979:173)

The land and family connection is a very real one and should prove most useful in understanding real estate investment behaviour. There is one final link, though, that needs reiterating before proceeding. In Beattie's discussion of T'un-ch'eng county in Anhui Province, the patriarch of a leading family there is frequently cited for his views on both land and education. Patriarch Chang Ying (1638-1708) continually stressed the compatibility of farming and study and the importance of land in lineage continuity (1979: 150-51). Moreover, contrary to contemporary Western and much overseas Chinese thinking, Chang Ying sees the greatest virtue of land as its inherent illiquidity. One's inability to liquidate land assets at any point in time is viewed by most modern investors as a negative attribute of landholding. For Chang Ying with his concern with maintenance of his lineage, just the reverse is the case:

The real advantage of land lies in its being difficult to sell in a hurry. If it were easy to sell then it would be a very simple matter to let it slip out of your hands. This is something which I have come to see in my later years but it was not at all the same when I was young. I say all this as a result of great and bitter experience. (1979:151)

However, as Omohundro (1981:145-46) noted earlier, this acquisition of wealth (or land in the present context) cannot but be a relatively brief interlude in the ebb and flow of family fortunes. In a system without primogeniture, where males of each generation share in the family's wealth (the land primarily in agrarian historical China), male progeny outstrip the ability of the family to increase landholdings and maintain their social and economic position. Thus, over time, despite Chang Ying's words to the contrary, family holdings grow and dissipate with succeeding generations. The vicissitudes of family status and wealth also kept the family unit sharp and poised over the ages to reassert periodically its ascendancy, paving the way for the economic vigour that has come to typify overseas Chinese business activities up to the present time.

What this process of rise and fall in family fortunes meant was a society like a seething cauldron, with families bubbling to the top only to burst and sink back to the bottom. When they burst they shattered their land-holdings too, and the patch-work quilt effect caused by the constant fragmentation and re-agglomeration of land-holdings was a distinctive feature of the Chinese landscape. This very process of constant flux within families, while at the same time each family was fiercely competitive with others around it, ensured a kind of social control through a fluid balance of power. (Baker, 1979:133-34)

Given the great importance the Chinese everywhere attach to their culture and traditions, it was essential to begin with an examination of the principal traditions and institutions that have an impact on overseas Chinese communities and on their real estate investment behaviour in particular. A broad range of elements, both of overseas and of traditional Chinese culture, has occupied the previous discussions. For present purposes, the most relevant were: the family; business and economic activity and culture; education; land; social and economic cohesiveness and distinctiveness; and uncertainty and fear concerning the future of Nanyang Chinese communities and their wealth and influence.

These elements are not readily separated. In fact, there are extremely close ties between the traditional family and Chinese business competitiveness. Both of these in turn are closely related to the legendary Chinese thirst for education. Finally, all of these elements can not be readily separated from both the historical institution of land and property in China and the present-day needs for acquiring and sustaining wealth by overseas Chinese family units as they seek to continue their family line and kinship relations.

Behind all of these connections and complexities is the threat of being uprooted and/or discriminated against or, in the extreme, facing physical violence. This fear, when combined with the overpowering Chinese desire to provide for succeeding generations and with their extraordinary business ties that transcend international boundaries, yields an environment within which capital flows and investments are likely to take place across national borders. Business know-how and connections provide the sufficiency conditions for these flows, while fear provides the necessary condition. In other words, fear and discrimination motivate the overseas Chinese to look around the Pacific Rim for stable investment opportunities, while the complex web of family, friends, and business linkages make it possible to make such transnational investments safely and wisely.

4

The Present Study: Its Method and Findings

It is impossible to comprehend fully the nature of overseas Chinese real estate investment behaviour in isolation. Rather, it must be set in context. Two contexts are of particular interest and importance. First, the overwhelming majority of overseas Chinese reside in Southeast Asia. Thus, overseas Chinese investment capital must initially be viewed as being integrally related to the extraordinary economic growth of this region. The recent economic performance there provides the basic economic fuel for overseas Chinese wealth and capital accumulation. Without this underlying economic record, it is doubtful that the Chinese could have accumulated the necessary capital to invest in real estate markets on the scale that they have.

Having established this macroeconomic environment, it was then necessary to develop the second essential context, namely the microenvironment of overseas Chinese communities. In the development of this context, it became obvious that there were a number of interconnections among aspects of overseas Chinese communities that could not be readily or fruitfully separated. Thus, education, business values, and success and the desire to perpetuate the family through time were inextricably linked. There was one other element that played a central role in the discussion of overseas Chinese culture and values — the institution of property and, more particularly, the enormous importance attached to land ownership and its close tie to education. Thus, a final broad linkage was established between land, the family, Chinese business enterprise, and education.

To take the argument to its next step, this chapter starts by sketching briefly the method that was followed to study overseas Chinese and their real estate investment activity around the Pacific Rim. The findings are the results of nearly eighty interviews carried out with leading overseas Chinese real estate investors and the financial and real estate experts who advise and serve them.

Initially, it was hoped that there would be sufficiently detailed information to allow a rigorous and quantitative academic analysis of capital flows among Pacific Rim countries, identified both by country of origin and destination and by source and use of funds. While such an analysis is possible within Canada (or the United States for that matter), it quickly became obvious that no such data source existed. Moreover, it became clear that there were virtually no hard data available on the subject of Pacific Rim capital flows for real estate purposes, let alone any detail on such flows from overseas Chinese sources. No comprehensive picture exists of such capital movements around the Pacific, although there are several "guestimates" for specific cities and regions such as Cutler's (1975) and Shulman's (1984) for Canada in general and Vancouver in particular, Daly's (1982) estimates for Sydney, Australia, Thrift's (1983) summary of Asian real estate investment in Australia (notably Sydney and Melbourne), and finally Zagaris's (1980) and Barak's (1981) figures of Asian investment in U.S. real estate. A recent paper by Apgar (1984) does suggest that overseas Chinese are still minor players in U.S. real estate markets compared with such massive foreign investors as the Europeans, Canadians and Middle Easterners.

An alternative research strategy, therefore, was called for. The first element was to develop as detailed a review of the existing relevant literature as possible. This review confirmed that there was in fact a marked absence of hard data as well as a relative paucity of serious research. There was no paucity of journalistic detail, indicating considerable public interest in the topic. While useful in providing background on real estate market conditions and the general economic environments that existed around the Pacific Rim, such material could not yield the required hard evidence or in-depth analysis.

In view of the lacunae in extant research and data, it was decided to interview Asian investors directly and also to speak with their North American and Southeast Asian real estate agents, valuers, and other business contacts. After detailed discussions with colleagues and, with business people involved in Asian property markets and after a review of the literature, a structure was arrived at for these interviews. It appears in revised form in Appendix I and sets out the broad range of issues and details touched upon in the interviews.

Interviews began in December 1982 in Hong Kong with a number of people involved in real estate investment both in Canada and in Asia, including investors, financiers, and real estate agents. On the basis of these preparatory meetings, further discussion with colleagues, and a seminar where these preliminary contacts and findings were presented, an appropriate interview framework evolved. The final question structure was the result of this refinement process. This process of consultation also led to suggestions for cities to visit in Southeast Asia as well as additional information sources, including Canadian High Commissions and immigration authorities, given the observed link between immigration and real estate investment activity in Canada and the United States.

With the benefit of these beginnings, a decision was made to visit Hong Kong, Singapore, Kuala Lumpur, and Bangkok in May 1983. Contact was made with nearly forty individuals in these four cities in advance of the interviews. In all, more than seventy people were interviewed, roughly distributed as follows:

Hong Kong	35
Singapore	15
Kuala Lumpur	10
Bangkok	10

Later, certain interviews were followed up by correspondence, and several additional contacts made in Canada and the United States. The results of these readings, discussions and interviews form the core of this book.

Circumstances (social, economic, and political) vary dramatically in the four cities where interviews were conducted. As was evident from the early discussion of overseas Chinese origins, the four cities and their respective nations (Hong Kong excepted, of course) drew their Chinese populations from different parts of China. Thailand overwhelmingly received emigrants from northeast Guangdong (Teochiu speaking people from the Swatow region), while Hong Kong is dominated by Cantonese speakers from southern Guangdong. Singapore and Malaysia, in contrast, drew large proportions of their Chinese population from southern Fujien province (Hokkien speakers). The widely varying regional backgrounds of the overseas Chinese in the four cities imply major differences in business and social practices.

Additionally, the overseas Chinese in the four cities have been subjected to different pressures and uncertainties and therefore find themselves living in widely varying circumstances. In Hong Kong, people face the expiry of the lease to the New Territories in 1997 and all the uncertainty that will accompany transferring the Crown Colony to the People's Republic of China. The recently signed accord between the United Kingdom and China has eased stress somewhat but has not eliminated it. (See, for example, Lau in the *Far Eastern Economic Review*, 25 October 1984, p. 18). Singapore, a tiny nation state, faces the threat of military invasion by its neighbours and the economic threat of heightened competition from around the globe. With no natural resources, miniscule land mass (roughly 650 square kilometres), and a history of difficulties with its nearest neighbours (Indonesia and Malaysia), Singapore must rely on its wits. Internally, it is relatively homogeneous with ethnic Chinese accounting for approximately 80 per cent of the island state's population. Despite the dominance of the Chinese, it is faced with considerable pressure to maintain equality for the large Indian and Malaysian minorities in the country.

In Malaysia, overseas Chinese face a different situation. They are in the minority, comprising between 35 and 38 per cent of the total Malaysian population. However, they face significant discrimination through the New Economic Policy which requires 30 per cent bumiputra (Malaysian native people) ownership of corporate wealth by 1990, independent of the amount of bumiputra capital or entrepreneurship being invested. The Chinese also face potential religious discrimination since they follow either Christianity or Chinese religions and not the Malaysian national religion, Islam. (See Tasker, 1983; Coppel, 1982; and *Asiaweek* in September/October, 1984 for details.)

Lastly, the Thai Chinese represent the smallest group in percentage terms (roughly 10 per cent of Thailand's population of 50 million). They are also the most integrated group, having been in Thailand for well over a century. Moreover, in the 1930s, after the 1932 Siam revolution, the Chinese were subject to a series of repressive and discriminatory measures ranging from severe restrictions on Chinese schools to business quotas for certain industries (Purcell, 1965: 131-47). Enormous pressure was accordingly exerted on Thai Chinese to assimilate. At present, virtually all Thai Chinese have taken Thai names, speak Thai, are Thai citizens, and consider themselves Thai. Nearly a century of social and political pressures has essentially led to the absorption of ethnic Chinese into Thai society (Williams, 1966:90-92).

Despite these measures in Malaysia and Thailand, the Chinese of those countries have prospered and exert considerable economic influence and/or dominance. In the words of a Thai friend, when asked about the proportion of Thai business in Chinese hands, "Thai business is Chinese business." An overstatement perhaps, but as the following data demonstrate, this is a statement that certainly captures the essence of the Thai non-agricultural economy.

In their recent study of the overseas Chinese contribution to Southeast Asian economies, Wu and Wu (1980) provide a number of estimates that illustrate the importance of the overseas Chinese. They also provide some interesting information on Chinese enrolments in universities. In Malaysia, Chinese access to universities is restricted through a quota system; the quality of Thai universities is increasingly suspect; and the scale of Hong Kong post-secondary institutions is so limited as to preclude all but the most gifted and energetic. Singapore alone appears to provide a scale and quality of education at the university level to satisfy ethnic Chinese demands.

Table 5 provides estimates of Chinese capital in Southeast Asia from 1930 through 1975. It shows a fourteen-fold growth of such capital in four decades. The 1969 estimate is disaggregated in Table 6 to show the distribution both by sector and by country. The tertiary sector dominates such investment, undoubtedly because of massive overseas Chinese banking activity, followed by the secondary manufacturing sector. Primary activities (agriculture, forestry, fishing and mining) are less important, comprising less than 15 per cent of total ethnic Chinese investment in Southeast Asia in 1969. (Note these figures exclude Hong Kong and Taiwan and therefore considerably understate total investment in the region.) Table 7 provides another glimpse of overseas Chinese involvement in these economies by comparing the proportion of employment among overseas Chinese with that of the overall labour force. It is clear that the ethnic Chinese are much more heavily represented in the tertiary sector than is the overall labour force, Hong Kong and Singapore being the only exceptions in view of the large Western involvement in the financial sector in both cities through multinational firms.

This banking activity is of particular interest, both because of its magnitude and geographic scope and because of the business connections that it implies. Some idea of the scale of Chinese banking activities can be found in Table 8. Moreover, given the role of international finance in the evolving world city system, Chinese banking ties are likely to be of central importance when considering the broader international capital networks and the world cities they connect. By extension, this skill with financial matters should also be of utmost relevance in understanding the specific flows of real estate capital about the Pacific Basin.

More specific detail is available when the focus is changed from the region at large to look at Malaysia and Thailand. This detail suggests a significant degree of control by Chinese in these countries over the modern sectors of the economy and over the education-based professions. Tables 9 and 10 give evidence of the control of assets by Chinese in Malaysia. Table 9 is straightforward and needs no elaboration other than to note that the Chinese accounted for 92.2 per cent of all non-corporate industrial fixed assets. Table 10 gives a similar picture, this time by looking at share capital. In some sectors, construction and transportation, Chinese ownership exceeds all others.

TABLE 5
SELECTED ESTIMATES OF CHINESE CAPITAL IN SOUTHEAST ASIA
(CURRENT US$ MILLION)

	Vietnam	Cambodia	Laos	Thailand	Malaysia and Singapore	The Philippines	Indonesia	Burma	Total
Shozo Fukuda (1930)	126.9	—	—	251.3	264	101.3	333.3	—	1,077.4
H.G. Callis (1937)	80	—	—	100	200	100	150	14	644
China Yearbook (1948)	0.5	—	—	212.8	1,761.3	—	550.3	100.5	2,625.4
Wu Ku (1960)	150	—	—	600	1,200	400	900	70	3,320
Yu Chung-hsun (1968)	80	—	—	700	1,200	500	400	50	2,930
Ho I-wu (1969)	430	55	40.1	412	1,470	573.5	704	135	3,819.6
Wu and Wu (1975)	—	—	—	3,737	7,845	1,289	2,570	—	15,441

Source: Wu and Wu, 1980:32.

TABLE 6
TOTAL CHINESE CAPITAL INVESTMENT IN SOUTHEAST ASIA, 1969
(VALUE IN US $MILLION)

	Thailand		Malaysia		The Philippines		Indonesia		Singapore		South Vietnam		Cambodia		Burma	
	Value	%	Value	%	Value	%	Value	%	Value	%	Value	%	Value	%	Value	%
Primary	73.0	17.7	250.0	35.7	10.0	1.7	—	—	70.0	9.0	100.0	23.3	5.0	9.1	—	—
Secondary	125.0	30.3	150.0	21.4	288.7	50.4	230.0	32.7	200.0	26.0	150.0	34.8	10.0	18.2	50.0	37.0
Tertiary	214.0	52.0	300.0	42.9	274.7	47.9	474.0	67.3	500.0	65.0	180.0	41.9	40.0	72.7	85.0	63.0
Total	412.0	100.0	700.0	100.0	573.4*	100.0	704.0	100.0	770.0	100.0	430.0	100.0	55.0	100.0	135.0	100.0

*The figure for the Philippines includes as Chinese only those who are not citizens

	Total ASEAN		Total Southeast Asia	
	Value	%	Value	%
Primary	403.0	12.76	508.0	13.44
Secondary	993.7	31.45	1,203.7	31.85
Tertiary	1,762.7	55.79	2,067.7	54.71
Total	3,159.4	100.0	3,779.4	100.0

Source: Wu and Wu, 1980:33.

TABLE 7
DISTRIBUTION OF THE OVERALL LABOUR FORCE AND OF CHINESE EMPLOYMENT

	Thailand 1969	(1957)	The Philippines 1972	(1957)	Indonesia 1971	(1940)	Malaysia 1975	(1975)	Singapore 1975	(1973)	Hong Kong 1971	(1971)	Burma 1973	(–)
Primary	78.1	(8.0)	54.2	(–)	60.5	(30.8)	59.2	(26.4)	0.5	(0.4)	4.0	(4.0)	66.3	(–)
Secondary	4.6	(22.0)	11.1	(11.5)	22.2*	(20.0)	15.2	(32.1)	35.1	(45.3)	48.0	(53.9)	7.0	(–)
Tertiary	17.3	(70.0)	34.6	(88.5)	17.2	(49.2)	25.6	(41.5)	64.4	(54.2)	48.0	(42.1)	26.7	(–)
Total	100.0	(100.0)	100.0†	(100.0)	100.0†	(100.0)	100.0	(100.0)	100.0	(100.0)	100.0	(100.0)	100.0	(–)

Notes: The Chinese employment figure and years of data are given in parentheses.

*The Indonesian manufacturing sector accounts for 7.5 percent of the labour force.
†Components do not add up to 100 because of rounding.

Source: Wu and Wu, 1980:38.

TABLE 8
ETHNIC-CHINESE BANKS IN HONG KONG AND ASEAN, 1979

Location of Head Office	Total No.	Banks with Foreign Branches (Based on Location of Head Office)	Private and Commercial Banks Wholly or Partially Owned by Ethnic Chinese Location of Overseas Branches											
			Sing.	H.K.	Mal.	Indo.	Phil.	Thai.	Taiwan	U.S.	U.K.	Japan	Other	Total
Singapore	14	6	–	7	64	–	–	1	–	–	3	3	1	79
Hong Kong	24*	16	1	–	1	–	–	2	–	9	3	3	1	20
Malaysia	19	4	31	–	–	–	–	1	–	–	–	–	–	32
Indonesia	44	–	–	–	–	–	–	–	–	–	–	–	–	–
Thailand	12	2	1	2	1	1	–	–	1	1	1	2	–	10
Philippines	11	2	–	–	–	–	–	–	1	1	–	–	–	2
Total	124	30	33	9	66	1	–	4	2	11	7	8	2	143

*Excluding thirteen PRC-controlled banks.

Source: Wu and Wu, 1980:99

TABLE 9

OWNERSHIP OF ASSETS IN MODERN AGRICULTURE AND INDUSTRY – PENINSULAR MALAYSIA, 1970

	Modern Agriculture* Corporate Sector		Planted Acreage Noncorporate Sector		Industry** (Fixed Assets) Corporate Sector		Noncorporate Sector	
	Thousands of acres	Percentage	Thousands of acres	Percentage	$M Million	Percentage	$M Million	Percentage
Malaysians								
Malays	5.0	0.3	349.3	47.1	11.2	0.9	3.9	2.3
Chinese	457.0	25.9	243.3	32.8	342.3	26.2	158.0	92.2
Indians	4.9	0.3	10.1	1.5	0.1	0.0	2.3	2.3
Others	48.1	2.7	13.2	1.8	187.2	14.3	1.4	0.8
Government	—	—	17.0	2.3	17.5	1.3	—	—
Total Malaysians	515.0	29.2	697.6	94.1	559.7	42.8	167.2	97.6
Non-Malaysians	1,249.6	70.8	44.0	5.9	747.3	57.2	4.1	2.4
Total	1,764.6	100.0	741.6	100.0	1,307.0	100.0	171.3	100.0
Percentage of Total Planted Acres/Fixed Assets	70.4		29.6		87.4		12.6	

* Modern agriculture covers estate acreage under rubber, oil palm, coconut, and tea. Ownership is indicated in terms of total planted acreage.

**The industry sector covers manufacturing, construction, and mining. Ownership is stated in terms of fixed assets.

†Government ownership of seventeen thousand acres in modern agriculture is included in the noncorporate sector, while the ownership of $M17.5 million of fixed assets in industry is included in the corporate sector.

Source: Wu and Wu, 1980:56.

TABLE 10
OWNERSHIP OF SHARE CAPITAL OF LIMITED COMPANIES,
BY RACE AND INDUSTRIAL SECTOR – PENINSULAR MALAYSIA, 1970

	Malay		Chinese		Indian		Foreign		Totals*	
	$M	%	$M	%	$M	%	$M	%	$M	%
Agriculture, forestry, and fisheries	13,724	0.9	177,438	22.4	16,191	0.1	1,079,714	75.3	1,432,400	100
Mining and quarrying	3,876	0.7	91,557	16.8	2,488	0.4	393,910	72.4	543,497	100
Manufacturing	33,650	2.5	296,363	22.0	8,880	0.7	804,282	59.6	1,348,245	100
Construction	1,258	2.2	30,855	52.8	447	0.8	19,937	24.1	58,419	100
Transportation and communications	10,875	13.3	35,498	43.4	1,903	2.3	9,845	12.0	81,887	100
Commerce	4,715	0.8	184,461	30.4	4,711	0.7	384,549	63.5	605,164	100
Banking and insurance	21,164	3.3	155,581	24.3	4,434	0.6	332,790	52.2	636,850	100
Others	13,349	2.3	220,330	37.8	13,348	2.3	182,862	31.4	582,516	100
Total	102,611	1.9	1,192,083	22.5	52,402	1.0	3,207,889	60.7	5,288,978	100

*Totals include share capital ownership by federal and state governments and statutory bodies and other Malaysian residents (individuals and nominee and locally controlled companies), amounting to about $M734 million. The racial shares in each sector exclude these two groups.

Source: Wu and Wu, 1980:55.

Three other measures of the importance of the Chinese in the Malaysian economy come from Tables 11, 12, and 13. Table 11 shows the dominance of the Chinese in scientific and technical positions in government in 1962.

TABLE 11
NUMBER OF SENIOR MEMBERS IN GOVERNMENT SERVICE
IN WEST MALAYSIA, 1962

	Civil Service	Medical Service	Educational Service
Malay	219	78	74
Chinese	17	347	131

	Technical and Professional	
	Scientific Background	Nonscientific Background
Malay	183	115
Chinese	539	176

Source: Wu and Wu, 1980:36.

TABLE 12
DISTRIBUTION OF STUDENTS AT THE UNIVERSITY OF MALAYA, 1971-72,
BY FACULTY AND RACE
(PERCENTAGE)

Faculty	Malays	Chinese	Indians	Others	Total
Arts	69.33	20.21	9.06	1.40	100.00
Economics and administration	40.15	45.85	12.70	1.22	100.00
Education	35.31	50.77	12.78	1.14	100.00
Pre-Engineering	6.12	89.52	3.94	0.44	100.00
Engineering	2.33	90.69	2.33	4.65	100.00
Agriculture	38.98	53.01	7.83	0.28	100.00
Medicine	24.01	62.53	11.92	1.54	100.00
Sciences	10.24	81.43	7.44	0.21	100.00

Source: Wu and Wu, 1980:36.

TABLE 13
MEAN HOUSEHOLD INCOME ($M) (1970 AND 1976)
AMONG MAJOR ETHNIC GROUPS IN MALAYSIA

	1970	1976	Average Annual Increase
		(in 1970 prices)	(percent)
Ethnic Group			
Malay	172	246	7.0
Chinese	394	612	9.1
Indian	304	378	4.0
Others	813	918	2.1
All	264	375	6.9
Area			
Urban	428	642	8.1
Rural	200	286	7.0

Source: Pang Eng Fong, "Race, Income Distribution, and Development in Singapore and Malaysia," in Lim and Gosling (1983), p. 321.

Table 12 suggests that such domination would be even more obvious today given that the 1971-72 Chinese enrolments at the University of Malaya were focussed on the scientific and technical areas. Table 13 provides a summary of this economic dominance by showing Chinese incomes are 2½ times those of Malays and growing more rapidly.

In Thailand, a not too different story emerges. Table 14 shows as of 1972 Chinese investment by sector and the percentage of total Thai assets by sector owned by Thai ethnic Chinese. As in Malaysia, only in primary activities are Chinese firms insignificant. In commercial ventures, the Chinese dominate the picture with roughly 90 per cent of the capital. The same is true in manufacturing. Banking and finance are only 50 per cent Chinese, largely because of massive government involvement here to keep the Chinese banks at bay.

TABLE 14
CHINESE INVESTMENT IN THAILAND, BY SECTOR, 1972

Sector	Number of Firms	Capital ($ Million)	Ethnic-Chinese Capital as Percentage of Total in Thailand
Commerce			
Import and export	1,000	500.0	95
Wholesale and retail	5,000	200.0	90
Restaurant	2,500	150.0	95
Service	500	100.0	80
Entertainment	150	50.0	70
Medicine	1,000	30.0	80
Transportation	10	1.0	80
Other	500	5.0	90
Banking and finance	50	300.0	50
Manufacturing	2,000	300.0	90
Agriculture	100	0.5	2
Mining	50	2.0	30
Fishery	100	1.0	20
Total	12,960	1,640.5	

Source: Wu and Wu, 1980:71.

Chinese business really is business in Thailand. In the late 1970s, it was estimated that 79 per cent of the students in Thailand's two leading universities were of Chinese or mixed Thai and Chinese parentage (Wu and Wu, 1980:31). This suggests that Thai Chinese will continue to exert extraordinary influence over Thai economic matters in the future. This Chinese preponderance in university enrolments, however, understates the Thai Chinese investment in children and education since it excludes the numerous Thai Chinese who study abroad in the United States and to a lesser extent in Canada.

Given the previously discussed differences in the Chinese communities of Hong Kong, Singapore, Malaysia, and Thailand and the widely different background environments in each place, the results of the interviews are reported city-by-city. Thus it will be clearer that different factors impinge on real estate investment behaviour in each.

1. HONG KONG: BORROWED PLACE, BORROWED TIME ON RECALL[3]

Hong Kong investor thinking has been so dominated recently by the lease renewal question that it was virtually impossible to separate investor behaviour from that all-pervasive issue. The first visit to conduct interviews in Hong Kong in December 1982 followed closely on the heels of Mrs. Thatcher's abortive visit of September 1982, while the May 1983 visit, during which the bulk of the interviews were conducted, corresponded to the precipitous fall of the Hong Kong dollar, the continued plummeting of stock prices (especially property shares), and the further slide of the property market (Hong Kong Rating and Valuing Department, 1983; Lethbridge, 1980; Youngson, 1982; and Yung, 1982). All in all, this was a gloomy setting within which to assess investor behaviour, particularly in real estate. Overseas Chinese are not new to making investment decisions in periods of uncertainty and fear. Despite this past experience, the lease issue has caused considerable upset among the less wealthy and has affected their unique Hong Kong lifestyle (King and Lee, 1981).

Nonetheless, most of the people interviewed had been through severe downturns before, and they were able to look beyond the short-run calamity to the longer run. The result was a set of responses that both reflects short-term fears and economic uncertainty and a longer-term view based on the need to diversify and preserve assets. In short, there is a set of responses that reflects the same trade-offs earlier seen impinging on overseas Chinese family businesses: short-term profits and long-term maintenance of the family unit. The closing chapter summarizes the interview results to place them in the broader context of present economic and political realities. At this point, those more general and imponderable issues must be set aside temporarily to review the findings of the interviews.

For consistency and to assist in comparison among the four cities, the findings are organized under the following four headings:

A. Investment Flows and Their Origins and Destinations
B. Investment Criteria
C. Information Sources and Methods of Analysis and Evaluation
D. Methods of Investing

The most interesting of these are the first three, since they varied most dramatically and turned up some of the most surprising insights. In contrast, it turned out that there was relatively more homogeneity with respect to methods of investing. Also, it became quickly apparent that for all but a small proportion, assets were acquired for keeping and not for selling, and thus the selling of real estate assets was of minor importance.

A. Investment Flows

The first surprise came in the initial interviews, where at the outset it was stressed that real estate investment flows are anything but one-way out of Hong Kong. Subsequent talks with people in Singapore, Kuala Lumpur, and Bangkok confirmed this initial impression. Hong Kong was seen as an attractive destination for much overseas Chinese money within Southeast Asia. Taiwan, Singapore, and Bangkok were all sources of Hong Kong real estate investment, and it is fair to note that major overseas Chinese communities all around Southeast Asia probably were involved in real property at some time during the heyday of real estate market activity in the late 1970s and through the beginning of 1982 when the Hong Kong property market began its slide. A common explanation for this inflow was that Hong Kong was the place to make money (as distinct from North America, the United Kingdom, and Australia, which were viewed as places to keep the money made in Hong Kong and other Asian property markets). It is not unreasonable to expect future real estate investment inflow into Hong Kong when its property market recovers.

Looking at outflows, North America, particularly the West Coast, was the most frequently cited destination. New York and Toronto were seen as very attractive locations as well, but generally it was the West Coast, with its relatively easy access to Hong Kong, which was preferred. Australia, a popular destination previously, was seen as less attractive in view of restrictions through the Australian Foreign Investment Review Board (FIRB) on overseas real estate ownership. Australia also lost some of its glitter when it tightened its admissions regulations for overseas students (primarily overseas Southeast Asian ethnic Chinese) and thus restricted the flow of these students into its universities. Lastly, Singapore was seen as a most active real estate market and had attracted much Hong Kong investment in the face of its looming development of the Singapore Mass Rail Transit (MRT), then in the final planning stages and now under construction. Much of this enthusiasm for Singapore has cooled recently with the glut in hotels and office buildings that has lately become all too visible (Kaye, 1984).

B. Investment Criteria

Previously, it was noted that several people stressed that Hong Kong and the high growth areas of Southeast Asia (Fung-shuen and Mera, 1982) are the places to make money. The kinds of capital flows of concern here accordingly place less stress on capital appreciation and more on capital preservation (or capital conservation as it has come to be known). Overseas Chinese investors are not an homogeneous group by any means, and a word of caution needs to be inserted since different investors have quite different criteria.

The very largest investors, often in real estate or manufacturing, have a large diversification element in their investment behaviour and strategies. It may be argued that portfolio diversification is itself a form of capital preservation. However, portfolio diversification is distinguished from capital conservation in that the diversifying investor is not necessarily averse to taking risks but rather wants to ensure that the risks are relatively independent of each other, so that on average the portfolio maintains its value and in the best of situations grows. Certainly, in such cases capital is nicely conserved. Accordingly, larger firms or wealthier individuals and families see overseas real estate investment as very much a part of a portfolio diversification strategy.

In contrast, smaller investors (who themselves still might be quite wealthy by any standard with assets in the $CDN5-10 million range), and also many large investors are often less willing to take risks. Therefore, they will trade off considerable potential return for low-risk situations, whereas the true diversifier is willing to accept individual projects with reasonably high risk, since it is the risk and return characteristics of the total portfolio that provide risk protection. Smaller investors will place a premium, in general, on safety, and relatively low returns on investment result.

Looking at the time horizon within which the investments are being made, it is not unreasonable to generalize for both small and large investors, and note that investments abroad are almost always long term (10 years and longer). Thus, short-term profits will be sacrificed for long-term growth prospects and stability. This long-term view implies relatively lower levels of leverage ("gearing" is the Southeast Asian and British term) than would commonly be encountered in North America. Lower leverage implies lower risk and is certainly more suitable for long-term holdings and preservation of assets.

Over and above normal economic investment criteria relating to risks and returns, there is a complex array of non-economic criteria at work, particularly in Hong Kong, which are tightly intertwined with many of the cultural and historical issues concerning overseas Chinese in Southeast Asia. These are the most interesting decision elements, since they take on considerable coherence when seen in the framework of Chinese in the Nanyang (literally in the "southern ocean"), whereas they would otherwise appear to be quite irrational and *ad hoc*.

Among the most important non-economic factors is the presence of family in the city where the real estate investment is to be made. Friends and business acquaintances are also seen as being important. An unexpectedly central element in all this is the connection between education and real estate investment overseas, a connection that follows directly from the desire to invest, if possible, in conjunction with the location of family members abroad. Sending children to study abroad at the university level is almost a necessity in Hong Kong because of the lack of university space.[4] It is interesting in this regard to note again that both the United Kingdom and Australia have recently tightened up considerably and raised the costs of university education for foreign (largely overseas Chinese) students. This has angered overseas Chinese in all the cities where interviews were conducted and will quite likely have an impact on overseas Chinese investment plans in both countries. Several contacts in Hong Kong mentioned that having children at university encouraged personal visits, which increased familiarity with the potential investment destination. Also, quite often small real estate investments were made to house the children while at university and/or to provide foreign source income to pay for schooling and living abroad. A spin-off of these small investments was stated to be that they gave the children experience in doing business and managing their own business affairs. All of this is remarkably in keeping with the discussion earlier about inculcation of business values (Omohundro, 1982; Silin, 1972; and Wu, 1982), and about education (Omohundro, 1981; Beattie, 1979; Wu, 1982; Purcell, 1965, and Williams, 1966), both in traditional China and among the Nanyang Chinese.

It is particularly interesting to observe that one of the reasons given for interest in Canadian real estate was the enormous number of Hong Kong residents who had attended universities in Canada. An estimate by the Commission for Canada in Hong Kong puts the number of Hong Kong-based Canadian university alumni at close to 60,000 people (Shulman, 1984). Both Canada and the United States are seen as providing excellent university educations with little or no discrimination against Hong Kong residents. This was frequently cited as a reason for considering investment in both countries: it created a positive feeling among potential investors; it enabled the children to come to both countries for schooling, and thus it allowed parents to become familiar with real estate opportunities in the cities where the universities were located.

Political stability was another factor of concern, and here English-speaking democracies, particularly those with growth potential, were seen as superior locations. Canada, the United States, and Australia were attractive for this reason.

Immigration policy is increasingly of interest to Hong Kong people. With the 1997 deadline nearing, and despite the 1984 accord, many people are concerned about the future and see the possibility of emigration as being of central importance. At the minimum, having children establish themselves as citizens in a stable democracy is seen as an essential means for perpetuating the family unit. Here again, the United States and Canada are perceived in very favourable light since both have rather liberal immigration policies for so-called "entrepreneurial class" immigrants. Immigrants under this classification are not subject to normal immigration quotas and are considered instead on an individual basis. The possibility of landed immigrant status arising from admission under the entrepreneurial class is of growing importance to Hong Kong residents who fear their loss of independence should they become Chinese citizens in 1997. Establishing some basis for immigration through real estate investment does exert influence on the investment decision, despite the fact that passive real estate investment *per se* is not in itself an admissable investment for entrepreneurial class immigrants. Nonetheless, real estate investment is an appreciable factor and a reasonable financial hedge in any event.

Finally, there are a number of criteria that are neither strictly economic nor completely devoid of economic content. They are not central criteria, but they do matter at the margin. Tax treatment of overseas investors is important, and foreign withholding taxes and other specifics are of concern. Inheritance taxes, or death duties, similarly play some role, though apparently a surprisingly minor one, surprisingly minor in light of their potential threat to Chinese concern with perpetuation of the family line. Foreign ownership legislation is another matter of concern, for two reasons; first, because of its indication of attitudes toward foreign investment, and, second, because of the costs and difficulties in working within its regulations. Australia's Foreign Investment Review Board has been particularly energetic in the real estate field (Daly, 1982) and has caused considerable concern among Hong Kong investors as a result.

In reviewing the investment criteria, one would have to conclude that the most important criterion, particularly for small investors, is capital preservation and its attendant criteria of political stability and the presence of family and friends in the chosen location. Real estate, as opposed to manufacturing or trading, is seen as superior because it is relatively easy to manage (local professional help can be purchased for a reasonable fee), and it is relatively safe, not subject to strikes or input shortages, and does not require constant attention. Lurking on the periphery of all this is the possibility of immigration (emigration from Hong Kong) and simultaneously obtaining a university education for the children and grandchildren.

C. Information Flows and Evaluation Methods

Flows of information were as diverse and intriguing as the investment criteria. Many are also just as firmly rooted in Chinese tradition and culture. In contrast, analysis and evaluation of the information were quite straightforward, relying on rather simple rules of thumb and past experience.

Family members, friends, and business associates were by far the most important information sources. The earlier observation about the Lukang Chinese to the effect that one does not do business with someone he does not know is borne out here (De Glopper, 1972). Once again, education plays a significant part since the children (or other family members) studying abroad are valuable information sources in their own right. Moreover, visits to foreign countries to see family members provide additional opportunities for potential investors to make contacts and to see properties or merely to get the feel of the local or regional property market.

Real estate brokers play a relatively smaller role, though once contacts have been made, brokers move out of the general category of impersonal business acquaintances and into the category of business associates, *if* they have performed honestly and well. Virtually all interviewees spoke negatively about the "carpetbagger" real estate fairs that have been promoted in Hong Kong by offshore real estate agents during the past few years. It was felt that these fairs were unsuccessful and that only the most naive and poorly informed Hong Kong investor would be attracted through them.

There was one area where established real estate brokers were seen as having an important information role, and that was in the purchase of large properties. Knowledge about such properties is confined almost exclusively to brokers specializing in investment and commercial real estate; thus these brokers do provide vitally important information for potential large-scale investors.

Finally, one cannot underestimate the value of such periodicals as the *Asian Wall Street Journal* and especially *Asiaweek* and the authoritative *Far Eastern Economic Review*. One is consistently impressed by the level and accuracy of detail about Pacific Rim property markets and economic conditions that appear in these periodicals. Worldwide real estate agencies such as Jones-Lang-Wootton, Richard Ellis, and Colliers International also publish detailed reports on Pacific Rim property markets and the economies of the region. In this vein, one must acknowledge also the highly detailed analyses of the region's economic well-being published by the Hong Kong and Shanghai Bank's Economic Research Department. Taken together, there is a remarkable amount of information published regularly and available widely, not just about Hong Kong and to Hong Kong investors, but rather about all of the important property markets in the area and available to all interested prospective overseas investors in Southeast Asia and North America.

Trusted family, friends, and business associates, including local lawyers and accountants who are resident in the city where the prospective investment is located, play a central role in the evaluation of this information. Personal visits are also extremely common and a virtual necessity for larger and more complex transactions. All sources suggested simple investment rules for evaluating the information with a heavy dose of "gut-feel" and past experience. The highly centralized family and business organization (Ward, 1972; De Glopper, 1972; Omohundro, 1981; and Wu, 1982) are at work as well. This traditional family and organizational structure is well suited to real estate investments, since it relies on personal contacts and business skills developed in previous activities. Despite having sophisticated analytical tools available, or even children with specialized North American business education, decisions seemed to be intuitive.

This is a point worth a brief digression. In the previous chapter the discussion of family enterprise focussed essentially on the typical small family business. However, many of the overseas Chinese enterprises in Hong Kong and the rest of Southeast Asia are large. Some, such as Bangkok Bank and Siam Cement in Thailand, are the largest enterprises in their field in their country. Other huge companies, such as Hutchison Whampoa, are Chinese controlled, as is Sun Hung Kai-Merrill Lynch and the World Shipping Group, all in Hong Kong. Others stretch into the hundreds. The question is just how relevant and useful is the previous discussion about Chinese business styles where those businesses were typically small and many of the emerging overseas Chinese businesses are large, some already enormous multi-nationals. Moreover, with the return of educated children, it can be asked further how long it will take for the children, with their Western training and management styles, to replace the traditional Chinese family approach.

Despite the growing scale of overseas Chinese enterprises, despite their growing complexity, and despite the Western education, a family tradition built up over millennia is not likely to vanish within one generation. Rather, it was surprising to see the number of Harvard and Stanford M.B.A.s in their early forties, with important titles in large firms, who had no real authority. Tight control was exercised by the patriarch or the eldest brother. The model of the small firm detailed earlier seemed to fit these complex giant enterprises perfectly. Just how long such tight organizational forms and management styles can endure is an interesting and clearly open question. However, the overwhelming evidence from these interviews was that the "small Chinese family business" is alive and well independent of the scale of the enterprise. It is, however, an enormously important and interesting area for future study and researchers should begin to track the evolution of management styles as firms continue to grow and continue to be managed more and more by Western trained progeny.

D. Methods of Investing

In keeping with the safety motive and risk aversion criterion, low leverage seems to be generally followed. Only large and sophisticated investors appear to buy properties by using funds borrowed abroad. The reluctance to borrow is based not only on the desire to keep risks low, but also on the relative lack of experience in borrowing abroad and lack of familiarity with local banking customs and foreign bankers. Obviously, for larger and more experienced investors, the ability to borrow abroad increases considerably, although the desirability of doing so does not necessarily increase. Low leverage, long-term time horizons, and safety (capital conservation) typify the investments in overseas real estate.

The very largest corporate real estate companies, such as Hong Kong Land and Swires, are very different. They will set up foreign subsidiaries to handle their overseas real estate investments where they will use their normal rules of leverage and sources of borrowed funds (Thrift, 1983; Daly, 1982 and 1984; and Cohen, 1981). They are important because of their scale and prominence abroad, but such large corporations are small as a percentage of the number of investments being made in terms of the aggregate value of overseas Chinese real estate investments.

Two other facets of ethnic Chinese real estate investing are noteworthy. First is the ease with which funds can be transferred. Using telegraphic funds transfer (T/T), monies can be moved across international boundaries within hours. Second, once funds are moved abroad, they tend to stay abroad, building a larger capital base for additional investment in the long term. This differentiates these flows from most international investment, since the bulk of international investment is for diversification of income sources for portfolio purposes. However, since so much Hong Kong real estate investment abroad is for preservation, it is unlikely that funds will be repatriated to Hong Kong. They are much more likely to be kept abroad "for safekeeping."

Turning from the mechanics of investing (which as was shown are remarkably simple) to the kinds of investments being made, one is confronted by an array of real estate forms that have attracted overseas Chinese funds. Accordingly, it is not possible to characterize them simply, nor is it possible or fruitful to attempt meaningful generalizations. Rather, it is most instructive to set out, in brief terms, examples of the kinds of investments being made. These investments range from modest, single-family houses or flats to massive, multi-million dollar central city prime office buildings and associated shopping concourses.

Smaller investors only have open to them a limited range of investments, ranging from small houses, condominium units and parcels of raw land to syndicated limited partnership units in larger developments of all kinds. They will have neither the financial resources nor the technical expertise to become involved in larger investments on their own. When the budget constraint is dropped and the investment preferences of larger investors are examined, the spectrum of investment possibilities broadens considerably. Purchase of condominiums and houses is widespread, either to domicile children in school or else to have a place to stay when visiting children, relatives, or checking other investments or businesses. Larger investments include small, medium, and large regional shopping centres; office buildings of various dimensions; massive mixed-use office-retail-residential structures costing hundreds of millions of dollars; hotels and hotel-shopping-residential complexes; parking lots and parking lot companies with their associated central city and prime suburban land holdings; apartment buildings of different scales and whole integrated apartment complexes; and, of course, raw land, though typically undeveloped lots in prime central city or residential locations. Large-scale land acquisition was most uncommon, which is consistent with the capital preservation motive of these investors. Since raw land acreage is highly speculative and risky, with virtually no cash flow in most instances except as parking lots, this sort of real property was not seen as a prudent investment. This is not to overlook the fact that several investors mentioned that they had purchased vacant parcels, either in prime downtown locations or in prime residential areas, where they might later like to build a house either for themselves or for their children.

While the range of real property is wide, there is one reasonably strong generalization that can be made: independent of the scale and type of property, as a rule Hong Kong investors are cautious and do their homework before deciding to purchase. Site visits are the rule, and friends and family are relied on heavily both in identifying good investment opportunities and in evaluating identified properties. As a group, the investors are highly sophisticated, not just about business matters in general, but also about the specific details and peculiarities of real estate development. Notwithstanding this generalization, there are, even within this group of very talented entrepreneurs, more astute investors and less astute ones. Nothing in the foregoing or in the following discussion should lead the reader to conclude that being an overseas Chinese automatically resulted in the Southeast Asian investor making a killing. Given the low leverage that accompanied most purchases, and the care that went into seeking out properties and negotiating on them, it is safe to conclude that on average the investment performance was more stable than that for the more highly leveraged and often less prudent North American real estate investor, although here too care must be taken, since there are a number of North American real estate companies that performed well even during the most dire days of 1981, 1982, and 1983.

To sum up, all sorts of real property attracted overseas Hong Kong investment, depending upon the wealth and objectives of the prospective investor. As a result, it is not possible to speak about either the typical overseas Hong Kong investor or about any typical overseas Hong Kong real estate investment. All that is typical is the great diversity.

2. SINGAPORE: A RETURN TO THE AGE OF CITY STATES

In May 1983, Singapore was just at or a bit past the peak of its most recent real estate boom. Subsequently, the market has fallen sharply: hotel, office, and retail markets all are presently or else soon to be glutted (Kaye, 1984). However, two years ago there was concern, but not gloom, differentiating Singapore from Hong Kong. There was another basic difference between Hong Kong and Singapore, and for that matter between Singapore and the other cities of interest: it is the only city or state where the resident overseas Chinese are dominant and have significant control over their own political destinies. Singapore's sovereignty provides Chinese Singaporeans with a degree of self-assurance and security which was markedly absent in Hong Kong and also absent in both Malaysia and Thailand, where past and recurring discriminatory practices have been aimed at Thai and Malaysian Chinese.

In view of Singapore's unique position, overseas Chinese investment behaviour can be expected to be quite different from that just examined for Hong Kong. It is.

A. Investment Flows

Flows of real estate investment capital into Singapore were extremely large. Not only were Hong Kong people taking advantage of Singapore's rapid growth, but so also were Malaysian and Indonesian Chinese. The last two groups are located very close to Singapore, have many business ties there and invest in Singapore real estate accordingly. The education connection also looms large here, this time Singapore being the destination of Indonesian Chinese students, particularly, but also of ethnic Chinese from The Philippines and Malaysia. Indonesia, especially, lacks credible secondary schools and universities, and the proximity and excellence of Singapore's schools attract Indonesian and Malaysian Chinese in large enough numbers that the National University of Singapore has had to limit foreign student enrolments from these countries in the face of this enormous potential Nanyang Chinese demand.

Inflows of capital take all forms, from individual condominiums to massive hotel, office, and retail complexes. The Hong Kong investors were in the market for diversification and capital gains, while the Malaysian and Indonesian Chinese appear to view Singapore in much the same way that Hong Kong Chinese view North America: a stable and safe place to preserve and protect capital accumulated in less stable and potentially hostile environments.

Capital outflows from Singapore to date have been relatively modest, especially to North America. The investment that has occurred has been largely to diversify assets in the true sense of portfolio planning. Investments range from large office and hotel complexes to single condominium units to be used for visiting children abroad or for frequent business trips, exhibiting a diversity of property types and sizes not at all different from that just discussed for Hong Kong. Destinations have been, until very recently, either the United Kingdom or Australia. The U.K. has lost its glamour as a result of sluggish growth and its discriminatory and restrictive education policies. Australia is similarly moving out of favour because of the Foreign Investment Review Board and its own overseas education policies. Previously, Australia's relative proximity (six hours to Perth by frequent non-stop flights and nine hours to both Melbourne and Sydney by equally frequent service) and close business ties between Singapore and Australia meant that Australia was an ideal location for diversification. With the fall from grace of both the U.K. and Australia, Singaporeans are beginning to look to North America seriously. Preferred locations are on the West Coast because of the lengthy travel time.

B. Investment Criteria

Given the relative security and growth possibilities in Singapore, investment motives are quite different from those at work in Hong Kong. Diversification is the prime motive. All respondents said that Singapore was the best place to make money because of its long-term growth. They did, however, feel the need to diversify because of the small scale of the island state. A subsidiary reason for investing is "to put away money" for the future, a criterion which goes beyond diversification and is rooted in capital preservation and perpetuation of the family. A final determinant is "where the kids go to school." It was suggested that a couple of flats "were a good way to earn tuition for the kids, provide them with good housing, and give them a little experience to look after the investment." Absence of exchange and foreign ownership controls is also important. This works against investment in Australia, but very much for investing in Canada and the United States. Canada, moreover, was seen as an exceptionally safe place to live and to send children to university, compared with the perception of crime in big U.S. cities.

C. Information Flows and Evaluation Methods

Just as the kinds and directions of flows differed between Singapore and Hong Kong, as did the relevant criteria and motives for moving money, so do the sources of information. Given Singapore's greater distance from North America, information flows are somewhat more restricted. Previous population movements from China to North America established pools of friends and family, largely from Guangdong, and provided a good set of information linkages for Hong Kong people in Canada and the United States. Singaporeans, in contrast, trace their roots largely back to Fujien province and relatively fewer Fujienese moved to North America. Thus, Singaporeans lack the extensive North American networks of information that are typical for Hong Kong people and their Cantonese relatives.

Investment opportunities are brought to the attention of investors primarily by real estate brokers with international connections. Banks also serve as information sources. Family and friends, as always in Chinese communities, provide additional useful information. Newspaper advertisements of properties abroad are increasing, as are the real estate seminars that have so annoyed people in Hong Kong, but they both remain a minor element. It appears that no one information channel is dominant, but rather all serve different potential investors at different times in Singapore.

As for evaluation criteria, it was pointed out by several individuals that Singapore investors are much less sophisticated than are those in Hong Kong. Accordingly, even greater reliance is placed on intuitive and rule-of-thumb approaches to making decisions for real estate investment purposes. Several examples were put forward to illustrate the lack of proper research and analysis before Singapore firms and individuals invested abroad. In particular, several Singapore companies have been very badly hurt in the United States in their eagerness to get into West Coast markets without first developing adequate information sources and performing appropriate analyses. All this can be expected to change significantly as Singaporeans obtain more experience and become more familiar with the markets and the modes of analysis required to move into them successfully.

D. Methods of Investing

Because overseas real estate investment by Singaporeans is still relatively new, the methods for investing are reasonably conventional. Low leverage is again the rule, and T/T is the vehicle for moving the funds to purchase the desired property. Several people pointed to an interesting leverage rule which set the leverage as a function of the cash flow the investment could generate. Leverage was determined so that interest payments would be covered by cash flow. The calculation was therefore the reverse of the traditional Western approach which says, "what is the minimum the investor can put down and still get financing." Here the question is how much money must be paid in cash up front so that the resulting mortgage payments can be covered by cash flow from the property.

Lacking experience, Singaporean investors so far have taken simple approaches to overseas investing. Prime properties are frequently sought to minimize risk and maximize safety and for the ease of maintaining the investment. Again, as with Hong Kong investors, real estate is seen as an excellent overseas hedge because it is easy to manage through professionals and because, if well located and maintained, it preserves its value and can even appreciate over the years. The long time frame adds to the attractiveness of real estate as an investment for people in Singapore as it did in Hong Kong. The same variety of types and scales of real property are seen in Singapore as "typified" Hong Kong investment. In short, the whole range of real property opportunities was of interest with no apparent preference for any particular type or size of property. Different investors did, however, have preferences for different kinds and sizes of real estate, depending again on their financial resources and investment objectives.

3. KUALA LUMPUR, MALAYSIA: CHINESE ANXIETIES ARE GROWING

As the scene shifts to Malaysia, for the first time in this study one sees up close the kinds of problems the overseas Chinese have faced with respect to indigenes. Under the New Economic Policy (another NEP), there must be 30 per cent bumiputra (Malaysian indigenous people) ownership of Malaysian corporate wealth (Tasker, 1983). In many instances this has led to confiscation of Chinese wealth in functional terms, as Malaysian Chinese have had to take on bumiputra partners, at costs to the bumiputra that are far below market value, in order to meet NEP requirements. Combined with some restrictions on holding political office, with Islamic fundamentalism on the fringes of the Islamic state religion,[5] with quotas on Chinese students at universities, and with more general concerns about education in Malaysia and particularly education in Chinese language, one sees almost a prototype of the kinds of problems catalogued by Wu and Wu (1980:173-93) that the overseas Chinese minorities have had to cope with in Southeast Asia. To make things more striking, Chinese comprise roughly 35 to 38 per cent of the Malaysian population, and in this sense they represent a minority only in the most literal interpretation of the word. In fact, if one considers the Indian population and other minor ethnic groups represented in the Malaysian population, there is no one group that can claim to hold a strict majority (Purcell, 1965:223-28). Thus, despite their significant numbers and overwhelming importance to the Malaysian economy (or perhaps because of these very strengths) the Chinese of Malaysia find themselves having to be alert to heightened discrimination and threats to their continuity.[6] Against such a background, it can be anticipated that investment behaviours of Malaysian Chinese will differ from those discussed up to this point, reflecting the different conditions under which they live. Also, the Malaysian Chinese have different roots in China, originating mainly in Fujien (32 per cent) and Guangdong (Cantonese speakers from the southern part of the province are found in equal proportion — roughly 20 per cent from Table 2 — with Hakka speakers from northern Guangdong).

A. Investment Flows

Malaysia is the recipient of only very modest inflows of real estate investment. The flows that do come into Malaysia are largely from Chinese in Indonesia, Thailand, and Singapore. Recent restrictions on foreign investment have meant that investment over $M1 million must be approved in advance by the Foreign Investment Review Committee.

As for outflows of capital, they have largely been destined for Hong Kong when it was booming; for Singapore during its recent growth phase and because of its proximity and historical ties with Malaysia (and Singaporeans' business ties as a result); and increasingly for North America. Canada is relatively less known than is the U.S. as a potential destination for capital. American sunbelt cities seem to be preferred. Australia and the U.K. used to be important places to invest, but both are now on the wane. The U.K. is less attractive as a consequence of the new education, immigration, and citizenship policies. Australia has similarly lost its shine. North America is likely to grow considerably in importance, both the U.S. and Canada, as more and more attention is directed abroad and these countries continue to allow foreign capital inflows.

B. Investment Criteria

Diversification is the prime criterion in Kuala Lumpur. Accordingly, good locations are sought with minimum risk, yet with the possibility of capital gains in the longer run. Low leverage in overseas investments is a concomitant of such a diversification objective.

In light of anti-Chinese feeling in Malaysia, safety and security for the family is also a consideration, perhaps one of growing importance, though at present largely in the backs of people's minds. Safety and political stability are also called for because of fears of potential Vietnamese aggression and the possibility of Thailand succumbing to insurgents from Vietnam and Cambodia. Lastly, the perceived slight possibility of return of ideological rule in China, with resulting changes in Southeast Asian power balances, is a distant consideration.

Other criteria that were mentioned in several instances included immigration possibilities tied to investments. This was particularly important with respect to Australian investment. It reiterates the need to perpetuate the family, which once more is tied to education. Given the recent emphasis on Bahasa Malay language and the downplaying of Chinese language and education, there is a growing concern about the quality of education, and the need to send children abroad for schooling is once more linked to possible investments and also to immigration. This long-term consideration of getting children educated well (and in English) combines with long-term objectives of real estate investments. It is clearly designed to protect the ethnic Chinese family in succeeding generations from adversity in a potentially charged environment, such as Malaysia's could become. In this vein, a minor consideration was inheritance taxes since they worked against the long-term family perpetuation objective; thus they were a deterrent for some people investing in the United States and the United Kingdom.

The longer run nature of these concerns was stressed repeatedly. In the short run, it was felt that Malaysia presented the best opportunities for economic growth and prosperity (not unlike what had been repeated frequently in Hong Kong). However, the traditional Chinese inclination to think long run did imply looking abroad and employing criteria such as those mentioned here.

C. Information Flows

Again, unlike Hong Kong, where personal contacts abroad dominated information flows, Malaysian investors rely on a broad range of essentially secondary sources. Real estate brokers from around the world provide much information. So do bankers, especially employees of large international banks with their own real estate departments. Newspaper advertisements and unsolicited letters with information about overseas properties are becoming increasingly common. Both these sources are held in low esteem, since it is felt, rightly, that properties marketed in this way do not represent very good opportunities, and they were perceived as being marginal at best. "Good" leads come from brokers, bankers, friends, and business associates with whom one has good contacts. These broker and business ties seem to be the most important, which is quite different from Hong Kong, where family sources are so central. Family ties and sources are less important, since there are few Malaysian emigrants and therefore few family connections abroad.

As in both Singapore and Hong Kong, the real estate fairs (mostly sponsored by Australians in Kuala Lumpur) are held in low regard. Unless foreign brokers work with local and trusted agents, little gain can be had from coming to Malaysia.

Evaluation of information varies tremendously. Common to all investors is the need to visit the property personally to inspect it and to assess the reliability of the preliminary information presented to the investor. Larger and more sophisticated investors rely on more sophisticated tools and more detailed site visits and analyses. For most, however, simple rules of thumb are used. Given the low leverage that seemed to characterize all of these investments, there is little need to do much analysis other than to be assured that the property is well located and will maintain or increase its value. High downpayment goes a long way to ensure viability and minimize risks associated with real estate investments and thus obviates much of the evaluation process typical of real estate investments in North America.

D. Methods of Investing

Investments are carried out in much the same direct manner seen in both Hong Kong and Singapore. There is one difference in Malaysia since foreign exchange movements between $M10,000 and $M2 million must be registered. Above $M2 million, permission must be gained from the central bank to move money legally. This is apparently only a minor inconvenience, but it is a consideration nonetheless.

Funds are moved by T/T as elsewhere. Monies are left abroad and not repatriated, particularly given the exchange control situation and the possibility that it could get tighter. As with investors from other cities, foreign companies are frequently created using local nominees both for tax purposes and often for anonymity as well. Nothing especially complex or different was apparent, aside from the need to deal with foreign exchange regulations. For types of real property sought, as elsewhere there was enormous diversity with no "typical" investment discernible.

4. BANGKOK: THE CHINESE AFTER A CENTURY IN RESIDENCE

Thailand presents yet another setting within which the overseas Chinese live. After more than a century of residence, the Chinese have become well absorbed into Thai society. The last anti-Chinese race riots were in 1956 and are largely forgotten now (Skinner, 1960; Purcell, 1965; and Skinner and Kirsch, 1975). Despite their dominance of the Thai economy and their visibility, the Chinese in Thailand, while eternally wary, appear relatively secure. Aside from latent resentment by non-Chinese against their economic dominance of the country, the Chinese voiced some concerns about Vietnam and military threats, though interestingly, it was the Chinese Communists in Beijing, the bane of Thailand only two decades earlier, who were now often seen as stabilizers of Southeast Asian politics. It is not strange to find in this setting a relatively low level of overseas investment being given prominence, although several sources suggested that there may well be more importance to the subject than people were willing to admit.

A. Investment Flows

There are moderate flows into Thailand by overseas Chinese for real estate investment. The sources are mostly ASEAN countries (notably Indonesia and The Philippines), as well as some from Hong Kong. Outflows are more significant and are directed toward Hong Kong, although this has been slowed by the decline in the property market, the People's Republic of China (particularly into such special economic zones as Shenzhen in Guangdong near Hong Kong), the U.S. West Coast (Los Angeles and San Francisco most notably), and Vancouver in Canada. Australia was formerly a significant destination, but is less so now because of the aforementioned restrictions on foreign investment and education. The impact of education is interesting since this is the only country in the group that is not in the Commonwealth. Thus, it was all the more intriguing to find such value placed on getting children and relatives an education in an English-speaking country. Apparently, English education carries with it some special attributes relating to its utility in international trade and overseas business transactions as well as access to certain types of education, such as business administration, that are dominated by English texts and research materials.

B. Investment Criteria

Diversification is once again the prime investment criterion. It was noted by several contacts that risk and leverage were fine ways to earn money in Thailand. However, to retain income, putting money abroad in low or no leverage situations was preferred. As in other cases, diversification is closely allied with preservation both of capital and of the family line. Race riots of the 1950s, the Vietnamese Boat People, the nervousness when Vietnam fell, and past discrimination against Thai Chinese all leave subtle marks. Thus, the desire to find secure settings for surplus earnings is an important consideration paralleling normal portfolio diversification considerations.

Because of the relatively long tenure of the Chinese in Thailand, there seemed to be some interesting differences between older Thai Chinese, who have led rather sheltered lives, and the younger people, many of whom were educated abroad. The older generation seems more conservative and more interested in staying with those economic activities that have served them well. The younger and frequently foreign-trained generation was said to be more innovative. Both, however, agreed on the need to invest abroad, the older group because of memories of past difficulties, the younger cohort because of its ties and experiences abroad.

Schooling is a consideration as well, though much less important than was seen to be the case in the other cities. However, where children do attend schools, particularly universities abroad, these educationally based ties do come into play in the investment motive, since they serve to open up possibilities and contacts that would likely not have occurred otherwise.

C. Information Flows and Methods of Evaluation

Nominally, exchange controls make it illegal to invest directly abroad without permission. Thus, newspaper advertisements in Thai papers are not supposedly an information source. However, foreign newspapers and periodicals do provide a wealth of information on the existence of investment opportunities and of additional sources, mostly brokers of information about such opportunities. Brokers from abroad are quite active in Thailand and do develop some limited business from direct solicitation. Local brokers are relatively limited in their activities because the Thai market itself is small and does not warrant a very active or large real estate brokerage industry. By far the most important sources of information are business associates, friends, travel, and, again, children attending university abroad. Informal contacts and word of mouth appear to be the principal means for disseminating information about overseas real estate investment possibilities, as well as travel and first-hand visits to prospective investment locations. In general, the information gathering of the Thai Chinese is more informal and *ad hoc* than the information processes seen at work elsewhere.

Evaluation of the information takes similar forms to those discussed earlier. Visits to see the property in question seemed to be the most common means. Friends and family are also normally called in to help evaluate the data and the property. Often assistance from overseas bankers is sought as well. Simple rules appear to apply, such as, if the property carries itself with a large downpayment and if it is likely to maintain its value, then it should be purchased. All of this focusses attention once more on the preservation criterion, its attendant low leverage, and a very long-term investment horizon.

D. Methods of Investing

The mechanics of investment once again appear to be very straightforward, the only impediment being the exchange controls. In theory no money can leave Thailand legally. However, several sources stated that the spread between the official rate of exchange and the black market rate was at most ¼ per cent for large transactions over $US10,000 and that transactions in virtually any amount (well into the millions of dollars U.S.) could be handled in less than a day, indicating a vigorous black market and an almost completely ineffective system of exchange control. Once the funds were moved out of the country, they would be forwarded anywhere in the world by T/T as elsewhere. And, as elsewhere, properties from individual condominium units to office and apartment buildings are all considered as investments, depending on the resources of the potential investor, the location of the investment and its proximity to family, friends, and known and trusted business associates who could look after it properly.

SUMMARY

Several consistent themes emerge from this examination. First, there is great diversity in investment motives, though there is a general consistent desire to conserve capital, and investment in real estate in stable cities and stable locations where value can be maintained and perhaps even added to over time is seen as a means for achieving this desire. Second, virtually all types of property are being sought. Smaller investors of necessity have to focus on more limited investments in single-family houses or condominiums, but larger investors put funds in everything from individual condominiums to massive, centrally located office-retail-residential complexes. While specific investors have definite preferences for one type of investment over another, there is no "typical overseas Chinese real estate investment" that could be specified. What the interviews did highlight, somewhat surprisingly, was the remarkably close tie between real estate investment, education of children and grandchildren, and conserving capital to perpetuate the family unit, all in keeping with the explorations of Chapter 3 dealing with overseas Chinese culture and values.

One caveat is in order at this point. Nothing in the foregoing discussion should be taken to imply that all overseas Chinese are wealthy and actual or potential real estate investors. Despite the enormous attention given to overseas Chinese business acumen and accomplishment, it needs to be stated explicitly that the investors who are the subject of this study are a very small minority of the forty or so million ethnic Chinese living in Southeast Asia (including those in Hong Kong and Taiwan). Their visibility does attract attention, however, and great care must be taken not to generalize from these highly visible and exceptionally successful people to all ethnic Chinese whether they are residing in Southeast Asia, North America, or elsewhere.

5

Circuits of Capital, Lines of Communication and Networks of Cities: Connections, Connections, and More Connections

There are three tightly interwoven and important concepts that relate directly to overseas Chinese real estate investment flows. First, there is the idea of "circuits of capital" recently put forward by T.G. McGee (1984), which brings together a body of evidence and literature to support the notion that the world is increasingly being connected by well-defined pathways or circuits through which financial and investment capital flows around the globe.

Closely related to capital circuits are the information conduits that provide the background information and data with which international investment decisions are made. The importance of such information sources and lines of communication have already been addressed with respect to the overseas Chinese investors. However, these communication links and information flows are also characteristic of the larger and more fundamental internationalization of capital markets that is at present underway.

Third, and last, there is a set of connections that is integrally bound to the first two, and that is the network of cities through which all of this capital and information passes and is processed. The concept of the "world" or "global" city has been elaborated on by a number of people in a number of ways (Thrift, 1983; Cohen, 1981; Friedmann and Wolff, 1982; and Friedmann and Goetz, 1982). A particularly intriguing thesis, which represents in a sense the ultimate extension of the world city idea, is that posed by Jane Jacobs (1984a, 1984b), which is studied in more detail below. Jacobs asserts that it is, in the end, cities and not nations that create wealth. Moreover, it is the linkages among cities that drive national and world economies. In a world economy dominated by services and information, and not goods, there is a confluence of these three ideas. Cities are generators of information and capital. The connections between cities represent the conduits through which pass the capital and information (parallel and complementary as they are) that are such essential facets of the evolving economic order. These conduits are ties that bind the network of world cities together. Each of these deserves more study in its own right.

In describing the emergence of the complex and tightly integrated international capital networks, McGee characterizes recent trends in these flows as being comprised of three sectoral components and a geographic or spatial component:

> Sectorally three sectors characterize financial flows (capital) (1) Official Development Assistance such as bilateral grants (2) Private flows consisting of direct investment, bilateral portfolio investments, multilateral portfolio investments and export credits and (3) Grants by private voluntary agencies. During the period between 1960 and 1976 there has been a marked shift in financial flows from developed to developing countries, in that sector 1 has declined from 60.0% to 41.9% of the total while private flows have increased from 38% to 54%. (1984:9)

Looking at the geographic or spatial aspects of these sectoral elements, McGee continues:

> At the level of direct net foreign investment there is an international network of capital flowing into the Asian market economies dominated by the U.S.A., Japan, Germany, France and the United Kingdom. The role of the international banking system is crucial in this flow of capital. Its importance in the Asian region may be gauged by the dramatic increase in the number of international banks active in the region. For example in Singapore the number of international trading banks and investment banks increased from 60 in 1970 to in excess of 100 by 1983. Within the region there are also networks of capital that may be labelled regional networks in which the overseas Chinese (in particular) are operating mainly out of Hong Kong and Singapore....This network of capital is facilitated by a financial network in which overseas Chinese banks play a highly important role. (1984:9-11)

Once again, the Chinese connection comes to the fore. Shortly, it will be demonstrated that this connection is an essential facet of the other connections being explored in this chapter and that there is in fact a remarkably tight articulation of overseas Chinese enterpreneurship, circuits of capital and information, and world or global cities.

These emerging and growing circuits of international capital are closely tied to significant changes in the international economic order. Two forces appear to be at work. First, there has been a shift away from the production of goods to the production of services and to the generation and maintenance of the information base that is at the heart of the service sector. Second, there has been a dramatic change in the geographic pattern of production. Manufacturing is increasingly moving to low wage, newly industrialized countries (NICs), while higher level services and technological development (itself essentially a knowledge or information based service) are concentrating largely in developed countries and in their major cities. The world city network is thus closely tied to these major trends in the world economic system.

These changes have been called "the new international division of labour" (NIDL) in a study of the same name by Frobel, Heinrichs, and Kreye (1980). Their work, done in the context of change in the West German economy, is easily generalized to the changes in the world economy at large. Compared to the old international division of labour, which was rooted in the sourcing of materials and energy for production of goods within developed nations, NIDL is a response to several shifts in the world economy. Writing about the concept, and seeking to extend it, Cohen notes:

> In essence, what the NIDL represents is a system for production on a world scale in which even greater numbers of people are integrated into activities carried on by large international producers of goods and by international firms which service these producers. Both the work process and the facilities used to produce goods and services are organized according to the demands of firms operating in a world market. In many cases, this integration of production and corporate services on a world scale has drawn increasing numbers of people into an industrial and service work-force, greatly diminishing the importance of agricultural and handicraft production. (1981:288)

Within the NIDL, there has been, as Cohen suggests above, an enormous emphasis on capital flows and international financing both of productive investment and of international debt. There have been fundamental shifts in international capital markets during the 1970s and 1980s. Daly suggests three particular factors have changed markets dramatically over this period:

The volume of money in the system has grown enormously; this pool of money has become much more mobile than ever before; and the system has become remarkably volatile. These factors have acted in circular causative chains to link the economies of different nations more intimately than ever before. (184:1006)

Daly goes on to point out that the willingness to lend abroad by huge international banks, based as they are in developed countries, was directly associated with the NIDL and with the decline of manufacturing in developed countries. Thus, the NIDL was both an effect and a cause of the explosion of international credit transactions and the articulation of the present system of international circuits of capital. As lending opportunities declined domestically with the decline in manufacturing in developed countries, the large domestic, internationally oriented banks began to look elsewhere for loan situations. The developing countries, where much of the labour-intensive manufacturing had shifted anyway, were prime foci for greater lending, though developed nations were also targets to provide the gigantic banks with worldwide, geographically diversified, loan portfolios.

A central element in the NIDL is the materialization of the global corporation, the logical extension of the previous multinational form. Global corporations provide a bridge between the NIDL notion and the global or world city concept. Information generation and processing is at the core of the global corporation and its urban orientation. In his examination of worldwide corporations and their impacts on Australian cities, Thrift sets out the following characteristics to distinguish the true global corporation from its mere multinational "brethren":

First, because these corporations are so large and are organized on a global scale they have a fully developed internal market which has to be administered within the corporation. ... Second, these corporations are increasingly fiscal instrumentalities based upon the direction and delivery of corporate capital to the most profitable locations as quickly as possible (and, as a corollary, away from the least profitable locations at the same speed). Third, and as a consequence of the first two characteristics, the global corporation has a greater need to gather, communicate and interpret information. (1983:3-4)

The need to acknowledge and promote the communication and information base of economies is closely tied to the NIDL and the parallel development of the quarternary sector (largely information centred). The importance of information and its generation and communication cannot be overlooked by any economy. Even in phenomenally successful Hong Kong, the need to look ahead beyond manufacturing is a necessity. In a recent study, Kwok argues strongly for explicit consideration of the role of information and communication in Hong Kong, despite its past and continuing success as a manufacturing centre.

> Communication needs have two basic intra-urban effects. First, techni-
> cally it is part of the global economic evolution. Broadly called "Infor-
> mation Revolution," it expresses the recent transformation from production
> of physical output to production of information and service output. In
> major international cities such as New York, London, Paris, Tokyo,
> Singapore, etc., this evolution takes the form of office development
> boom. Offices are the production plants for information business and
> professional services. Typically, international cities are not dominated
> by chimney studded factories but high-rise offices. (1983:4-5)

As Kwok later points out, hardware and technological gimmickry are not sufficient to be plugged in to the world information net. More importantly, cities and nations must possess adequate pools of highly educated commu-nicators, analysts and processors of information, if they are to have any reasonable chance to "make it" as world cities. The education connection returns again in a different guise and in quite a different context to comple-ment networks of capital, of information, and of world cities. This evolving information and communication economy requires labour of an enormously skilled type. Out goes manual dexterity and brute strength, and in come technically trained decision-makers, analysts, and highly skilled managers. Such pools of talented professionals are both found in and largely products of urban environments. The education/city nexus is thus clearly established to be added to the other linkages developed with respect to the overseas Chinese, and it is connected firmly to these earlier linkages through educa-tion and the urban focus of the ethnic Chinese (1983:14).

At last the role of the city in economic change, and in economic growth, begins to be apparent. Cities are envisioned as the nerve centre of the evolving world economic order. Cohen places cities at the hub of the NIDL:

> Changes in the corporation and in the structure of the advanced corpo-
> rate services have led to the emergence of a series of global cities which
> serve as international centers for business decision-making and corpo-
> rate strategy formulation. In a broader sense, these places have emerged
> as cities for the coordination and control of the NIDL. (1981:300)

However, it is not the NIDL alone that is reshaping cities around the world. The structural shift in the world economic system away from goods production and toward services and information production/processing (which admittedly is itself inextricably intertwined with the NIDL) is having significant consequences even for smaller cities that are unlikely to be drawn into the vortex of global firms and global networks. Stanback and Noyelle, in their study of medium-sized U.S. cities caught in these great worldwide transition, suggest that the new service orientation has built into it an inseparable urban dimension, in marked contrast with much manufacturing industry of the preceding hundred years or so which has become increasingly footloose, non-metropolitan, and even non-urban in its locational requirements.

> Accordingly, growth of services has been strongly associated with the growth of cities, and the economic fortunes of many metropolitan places have been closely tied to their ability to accommodate to the service transformation. (1982:8)

Building on Cohen and the notions of the NIDL and the global corporation, Thrift focusses on the regional headquarters of these global firms as the key connections between world capital and information flows, the growth of global cities, and the networks that in turn connect these global cities. Thrift suggests two reasons for this bond between the regional headquarters of global corporations and world city growth.

> First, world cities are the chosen sites for regional headquarters offices. The presence of a number of regional headquarters offices is a good indication of whether a particular city is a world city. Second, the regional headquarters office has made it possible for the number of world cities to expand. ... Since the late 1960's the institution of the regional headquarters office has meant that a decentralisation of corporate power has taken place and within this decentralisation of power there has been a corresponding increase in the number of world cities. (1983:5-6)

A somewhat different view of the role of cities in the NIDL is provided by Daly (1984). His prime concern is with international capital markets and capital flows and their impacts on Australia and its cities. However, his observations can be generalized, and they cast the global city phenomenon in a different setting. To begin with, he sees capital flows and the international firms that need to move capital as being at the core of the global city. The requirement to move massive amounts of capital on a twenty-four hour basis across the international money market has led to the additional requirement of highly sophisticated communications equipment and equally sophisticated professionals who can interpret and act on the capital flows and the information about the ebb and flow of world economic conditions. In short, international firms, especially the huge international banks, need a set of complex and sophisticated inputs that can only really be provided by the largest and most advanced cities (p. 1009).

In Daly's view, these firms and their international capital movements are the basic underlying forces pushing for the creation of ever more global cities. In the context of Australia, it is the major cities that form the bridge between the national and international economic systems. Recent changes in Australian offshore banking rules[7] will make Daly's remarks even more germane today.

> Australia's link to that system is through its major cities, Sydney and Melbourne. Sydney is the dominant centre although Melbourne for most of the twentieth century was Australia's financial capital. The intrusion of foreign groups was largely responsible for Sydney's rise. By 1976 when S.I. Davis (1976) published a 'league table of international financial centres' Sydney ranked ninth in the world and Melbourne twenty-ninth. Ninety-five foreign banks and offices in Sydney in 1982; 45 in Melbourne including 16 with offices in both cities. (1984:1016)

Up to this point, attention has focussed on the city and its world variant as being the result of the forces of the NIDL and its attendant highly articulated international capital and information markets. An even more basic role is assigned to cities by Jane Jacobs in her recent writings, where it is the city that creates the economic order and not the other way round. Her thesis is an intriguing one with enormous consequences for the ways in which cities grow and for the policies that are designed to address both urban and national economic development.

As envisioned by Jacobs, the city, when stripped of other trappings, performs two functions to survive. First, it replaces imports with locally produced goods and services. Second, it foments new ideas that enable it to expand its exports. This expansion in turn promotes imports which in turn leads to substitution. In her words:

> The expansion that derives from city import replacing consists specifically of five forms of growth: abruptly enlarged city markets for new and different imports, consisting largely of goods from rural areas and of innovations being produced in other cities; abruptly increased numbers and kinds of jobs in the import-replacing city; new uses of technology, particularly to increase rural productivity; increased transplants of city work into non-urban locations as older, expanding enterprises are crowded out; and the growth of city capital. (1984a:44)

Looking at cities in this way, Jacobs zeroes in on the key function provided by currency. If left on their own, as is the case with such city-states as Hong Kong and Singapore, changes in the international value of the city's currency automatically provide a dynamic negative feedback indicating whether the city is doing things right or wrong. If the national economy is working well, the nation exports more goods and services than it imports, and foreigners, seeking to buy the nation's goods and services, bid up the value of its currency. If the nation is a net importer, then the currency is going to be bid down in value (1984a:54).

When robbed of the vital information provided by movements in the value of its currency, nations must necessarily become unstable. Since national governments deprive their cities of the right to issue currency, cities are also deprived of the vital feedback carried by exchange rates:

> One might say, except that it implies an undeserved censure, that American cities have suffered badly from lack of economic discipline: the discipline imposed by currency fluctuations, or, if we prefer, the opportunities presented by currency fluctuations. These can make it possible for a city's falterings to be merely temporary. But uncorrected, faltering becomes final. The failure is not the fault of the cities, the government, or the American people. It is a structural flaw that comes with the territory. We must be grateful that a world government and a world currency are still only dreams. (1984a:66)

In marked contrast to the decline that is imminent when currency signals are obviated through uniform national currencies, Jacobs sees a vigorous, flexible, and enduring process as the result of freely fluctuating city currencies. The on-going pressure to adjust the city-nation currency is the driving force in her view for the continuous innovation and adaptation that is characteristic of the successful and surviving city (1984b:113-14).

In summing up her argument, Jacobs notes that dealing creatively with the uncertainties and vicissitudes of city life is the only long-run solution to urban development or decay. Cities cannot rely on nations for handouts to deal with the fluctuations. If cities are allowed to decline and wither, then it is Jacobs's thesis that national economic decline cannot be far behind (1984b:114).

Recent ideas about international flows of capital and information have been woven together here with other emerging ideas about the network of global cities that both services and promotes these flows. The global city is thus both cause and effect of the evolving information economy and the NIDL. World cities are magnets of world capital and information. Thus, they draw these essentials unto themselves. World cities are also sources of information and capital for additional economic development and for the creation of even greater numbers of global cities which can be productively plugged into the global city system. Cities have a pivotal role in all this. If Jacobs's conjectures have any validity and value at all, cities should be seen as the progenitors of economic change and economic survival. Inherent in new international division of labour is the pressure which pushes cities onward to create new ideas and new work in their on-going striving to adapt and survive in changing economic times. In the global city concept, there can be seen an adaptive response to the changes wrought by the NIDL. Finally, the burgeoning international circuits of capital and information bind this complex of cities and new economic activity together.

In all of this, just out of sight, are the parallel and complementary networks of capital and information of the overseas Chinese entrepreneurs, who reside overwhelmingly in cities, provide further adaptive capability to the global city network, and to the lesser cities that tie into it. The connections delineated in this chapter mesh fully with previous findings about the overseas Chinese and their investment behaviours. In the case of the latter, they too seek locations with abundant educational resources, stable and broadly based economies, sources of information and capital, and other overseas Chinese: in other words, the global city.

This knowledge should not be seen in isolation from the evolving world economic system and the tightly concatenated global city set that is part of that system and of its emerging changes. Rather, this is knowledge that should be put to use to assist in adjusting to the new international division of labour and to the requirements of global corporations and global cities. In short, there are policy uses to be made of the findings and syntheses developed in all of the foregoing discussions.

6

Summary and Conclusions, Needing Extensions, and Policy Considerations

SUMMARY AND SYNTHESIS OF THE INTERVIEW FINDINGS

Trying to summarize and synthesize the foregoing findings runs the risk of blurring over important differences in the quest for useful generalizations. In some areas the risk is worth taking, while in others the differences are just too important to overlook. This becomes clearer when the four areas under which findings were grouped are examined. As a guide to the findings, a summary Table has been constructed to promote quick visual comparison (Table 15).

A. Investment Flows

Differences were so great here that it is not possible to make any meaningful synthetic generalizations. All that can be said is that each city had its own unique set of sources and destinations of real estate investment funds. The sources and destinations depended very much on business, political, and cultural conditions in both the originating and receiving area. Aside from this, it is not possible to be more specific without violating the differences that were highlighted in our discussions above. Diversity of origin and destination is the only general observation that can be made here.

TABLE 15
SUMMARY OF INTERVIEW FINDINGS

		Hong Kong	Singapore	Kuala Lumpur	Bangkok
Methods of Investing	Use Retained Foreign Earnings Abroad	1	1	1	1
	Telegraphic Funds Transfer	1	1	2	3
	Shell Companies	2	2	2	2
	Direct Investment/ Equity Ownership	1	1	1	1
Information Sources and Methods of Analysis	Direct Mail Advertising	3	2	2	2
	Financial Institutions	3	2	2	2
	Real Estate "Fairs"	3	3	3	3
	Mass Media and Magazines	3	2	2	2
	Real Estate Agents	2	1	1	2
	Site Visit/Inspection	1	1	1	1
	Trusted Friends and Business Associates	1	1	1	1
	Family (inc. Children)	1	2	2	2
Investment Criteria	Tax Treatment	2	2	2	2
	Location of Family, Friends, Trusted Business Ties	1	1	2	2
	Potential for Growth	2	2	2	2
	Ease of Access from S.E. Asia	2	1	1	2
	Linked to Location of Children's University	1	1	1	2
	Possible Immigration	1	3	2	3
	Capital Conservation	1	2	2	2
	Portfolio Diversification	1	1	1	1
Origin and Destination of Flows	Other (S. America, other Asia)	3	3	3	3
	Western Europe	3	3	3	3
	Other Southeast Asia	2	2	3	3
	Hong Kong	1	2	1	1
	Singapore	2	1	1	2
	United Kingdom	2	2	2	3
	Australia	1	1	1	2
	Other Canada/U.S.	2	2	2	2
	Western Canada	1	1	1	2
	Western U.S.	1	1	1	2
Place		Hong Kong	Singapore	Kuala Lumpur	Bangkok

Key: 1 = Very frequently cited   *Source:* Personal Interviews by Author
       2 = Frequently cited
       3 = Seldom cited

B. Investment Criteria

Here again, different cities had quite different criteria for investing abroad in real property. However, there are some useful generalizations that do seem to span all the cities visited. All of these criteria should be seen against a backdrop of age-old and continuing uncertainty and discrimination against ethnic Chinese communities in Southeast Asia.

a. Diversification was a key element in the investment decision to minimize portfolio risk.

b. Security was another common thread. People sought safe refuge for their funds where they could preserve surpluses earned domestically. Capital conservation seems a ubiquitous concern, no doubt tied to the perpetuation of the family.

c. Immigration was mentioned in all cities, though it was only of prime concern in Hong Kong and of secondary concern in Kuala Lumpur. Keeping open the *possibility of migration* for children and grandchildren, however, was virtually a universal response. Given the hardships faced by the overseas Chinese and present uncertainties, this criterion is obvious.

d. Tying investment to university education also turned out to be surprisingly important and surprisingly general. In all cities, respondents talked about the importance of having children at university and associated family available to assess information and look after the investment or the professionals who would be managing the investment.

e. Access was also an implicit investment criterion in all cities. The ability to fly to the location of the real property was an important consideration and explained, in part, why investors from different cities preferred different overseas locations (for example, Singaporeans initially to Australia, Hong Kong to North America, ASEAN to Hong Kong and Singapore).

f. Growth potential, in keeping with risk aversion, was also a common criterion.

C. Information Flows and Evaluation

While the relative importance of different sources of information and different means for evaluating this information varied from place to place, there were a number of general points.

a. Importance of family, friends and business associates in providing information and in helping to evaluate it was noted by all and stressed by most. The family was a key factor, as was education, since much of the information discussed is generated and evaluated by children or other family abroad at university. For non-family, the personal and particularistic nature of Chinese business practice comes through again as it did in our background discussions. It would appear that one does not do business with a stranger if at all possible.

b. Organized real estate organizations had a surprisingly large role in providing information. International organizations were especially respected, particularly those that worked through known and trusted local brokers. Again, the personal element is a key here and the ability to work with local agents is clearly a strong advantage everywhere.

c. Mass media such as newspapers and magazines provided an excellent source of information about general business conditions and about the status of particular property markets, and serve a useful, if limited, role (most notably the advertising aspects of these media).

d. It was a surprise to hear at least one respondent in each city observe that banks, either their own or international banks, provided both useful information and assistance with evaluating the information.

e. Site visits were noted by virtually all contacts as being a necessity. Most commonly the investor visited the site personally, but if that were not possible, then trusted family, friends, business associates, or employees did the on-site inspections and evaluations.

f. Finally, in those cities where foreign real estate agents had sponsored "fairs" advertising their wares, these fairs were viewed with suspicion and held in low esteem. It was felt little in the way of quality opportunities would be found, and the fair itself was seen often as demeaning.

D. Methods of Investing

Very few surprises were evident here. The methods were straightforward and similar using telegraphic transfer of funds (T/T) with the frequent use of local shell companies and nominees for tax purposes and anonymity. Malaysia and Thailand presented some interesting variants since forms of exchange control are in place in both countries but seemed to be far from binding in either nation.

When looking at the kinds of properties being purchased, diversity again summarizes the situation. Investors with more modest means were obviously restricted to smaller projects, usually single houses or condominiums. The largest investors also invested in these, but concentrated on the whole array real estate investments: offices, retail, apartments, hotels, and shopping centres. Scale varied from modest to massive. Thus, no generalizations are possible about the "typical" kind of purchase.

EXTENSIONS

Several extensions follow logically from this effort. First, the limited interview sample does hinder reaching more general and powerful conclusions. Accordingly, expanding the scope of successive studies appears in order. The scope can be expanded geographically by adding such countries as Indonesia, The Philippines, and Taiwan and such cities as Penang, Jahore Bahru, and Malacca in Malaysia and Chiang Mai in Thailand. It can also be expanded by developing additional contacts in the cities previously visited. Finally, conditions have changed dramatically in the past two years and are likely to change as dramatically in the coming years, so moving the study ahead in time would provide useful insights.

A second source of extensions deals with methodology. First, survey research could be undertaken in selected cities to try to ascertain the degree and importance of overseas Chinese real estate holdings and intentions (behaviours). Second, a number of detailed case studies could also be undertaken in different cities using different scales and types of investments and investors to try to glean more specific information about the mechanics and details of investment decision-making. Comparing across case studies would also lead to some helpful generalizations against which the present findings could usefully be assessed.

POLICY IMPLICATIONS

These interviews implied some very considerable scope for government policy to influence and shape the nature of overseas Chinese real estate investment in Canada and also in the United States. The recent removal of the Canadian *Foreign Investment Review Act* and its replacement with more liberal *Investment Canada Act* is illustrative of a policy change that is likely to encourage overseas Chinese investment in Canada. The following policy examples are rooted in the interviews reported on here. They are directed to Canadian policymakers, but they are usually relevant in the U.S. as well. Additionally, they complement the more general policies set out in Hofheinz and Calder (1982) directed to American business and government decision-makers to cope with the Asian "challenge."

To begin, Canada and the U.S. should continue to be as flexible as in the recent past in encouraging the entrepreneurial immigrant class, in order to attract leading overseas Chinese entrepreneurs not just for real estate development but, more importantly, for a broadening of North America's entrepreneurial and economic base.

Given the importance of education, each province or state should be encouraged to certify private secondary schools so that potential students have assurances that these are *bona fide* and good quality educational institutions. Canadian High Commissions should also inform overseas Chinese about the fees that can be paid for access to the excellent public secondary school systems in Canada. At the university level, wide access should continue and, if necessary, differential fees should be charged only for those who can afford to pay.

Lastly, greater access by air with Pacific Rim nations needs promoting to overcome some of the tyranny of distance represented by the Pacific Ocean. As well, prospective investors should be given as much information as possible about doing business in Canada through the trade commission services in Southeast Asia.

As has been noted, there are radical changes occurring in the kinds of goods and services being produced in the world economic system with a movement, in the aggregate, away from goods production to service and information production and processing. Attendant on this structural shift has been a geographical shift with three principal components. First, there is a sorting out of economic function (the NIDL), which sees newly industrializing countries playing a larger and larger role in the production of goods and materials, with the already developed nations providing the higher level services. Second, there is a marked urban bias in all of these activities, particularly in the provision of high level "producer" services, most importantly and typically financial and management services. Third, the Pacific Rim region is capturing a disproportionate share of the growth in world output.

Intermingled throughout this scenario, particularly as it relates to the Pacific Rim, are the overseas Chinese. As has been shown they play central roles in the economies of the region and are likely to continue in their functions as traders, bankers, risk takers, and, most importantly, as information transmitters and processors. In keeping with these emerging world economic forces, North Americans, and Westerners more generally, must place international economic activities in this broader perspective and be aware of the major shifts currently taking place.

TOWARD A BROADER TRADE POLICY PERSPECTIVE

While the specific policy remarks that follow are designed particularly for a Canadian context with its special foreign trade problems (largely stemming from the current natural resource base of exports and the manufactured nature of imports), there is much in the policy suggestions of use in the U.S. For example, tying capital investment and entrepreneurial immigration is as relevant in the U.S. as it is in Canada. The call for serious development of a West Coast international financial centre tied in part to overseas Chinese connections is also germane in the U.S. However, caution needs to be used in applying these prescriptions blithely to the U.S.

The policy view being espoused here for Canada comprises two parallel elements: broadening the conception of what Canada can trade and broadening the set of trading partnerships. The thrust of both discussions is that Canada requires more diversity both in the commodities and services traded and in the countries with which it trades, circumstances that do not generally apply to the U.S.

The prevailing view of Canadian economic development, revised and disguised and elaborated upon for most of the present century, is the staple theory (Marr and Peterson, 1980:10-18). In hackneyed terms, this view says that Canada is a provider of natural resources and of the semi-finished products based on these resources (for instance, lumber and wood pulp). Because of large resource endowments and high labour costs, it is argued that Canadians can best feed and clothe themselves by sticking to their traditional role as "hewers of wood and drawers of water." Present policy in British Columbia, while trying to move away from excessive reliance on resources, still sees the province largely in this role. Thus, enormous public investment has been made in such projects as coal development in Northeastern British Columbia. Such an approach has attractive short-run features. It does not provide, however, a very diversified economy that can take advantage of the alterations that are on-going in the world economy. Recent B.C. government interest in free trade zones, international finance, and high technology do suggest essential change in the wind. This traditional view also does not provide an accurate picture of the real nature of Canada's exports, which in fact embody every bit as much technology and know-how in resource exports as they do "natural resource endowments." In this sense, Canada is already an exporter of high technology. Coal is a useful example.

In Canadian trade statistics, a tonne of coal appears as a tonne of coal. From Appendix Table 13 it can be seen that British Columbia exported nearly $CDN 700 million worth of coal to Pacific Rim countries in 1982. However, embodied in that export figure is an extraordinary technological base that is not seen in the crude dollar figures. To export that much coal takes exceptional transportation technology and management procedures. Moreover, mining such a vast quantity of coal requires enormous amounts of invested capital, technology, and human skill. Finally, significant expertise in international finance and credit arrangements is also a prerequisite for such transactions. In short, the $700 million dollar coal export is really comprised of much more than just coal itself and includes great know-how in extracting, moving, marketing, and financing the export.

When viewed in this light, one sees that it might not be the coal at all which provides Canada with its trading advantage, but rather the whole underlying technological and supporting know-how. It might, therefore, be just as plausible to market the technology and ancillary skills as it is to market the apparent product, the coal. Under such a broadened view, Canada would have a greatly expanded marketing opportunity both for its coal (to end users) and for its technology and support services (for its prospective competitors). This view implies that Canada does not necessarily have to compete in only the world resource market, where the alternative suppliers are numerous, growing, and highly competitive, but that it also can compete in the much more restricted and selective world market for resource extracting technologies. This is much more in keeping with the structural shifts in the world economy (NIDL) noted at the outset of this policy examination and in Chapter 5.

Changing perspective, therefore, from exporting mere materials (for which substitutes and competitors abound) to the technology and support services embodied in these resources opens potentially vast new markets to Canadian firms in the resource field. Moreover, these markets for extraction and support technologies and services are much less competitive, much more likely to be more lucrative, and can significantly broaden the base of Canadian trade while removing it from some of the vicissitudes of periodically glutted resource markets.

Coal is one example, but analogous scenarios could be sketched for lumber and wood products, non-ferrous metals, and fishing and agricultural products and markets. In all of these, Canada has built up a significant body of expertise and technology which is as marketable as, if not more marketable than, some of the resources themselves. These comments apply to U.S. resource exports too.

This kind of thinking can be extended further, to look at the possibility of trading in services *per se*, independent of any underlying resource or product, moving Canada much more into the mainstream of current economic growth patterns as sketched in the "new international division of labour" and global cities. Such services as finance, insurance, and real estate would be, in fact already are, prime candidates for world markets. Other obvious candidates would include tourism, health care and health care technology, education and transportation and communication services and technologies. In each, Canada has significant expertise and rates among the world leaders.

The second area in which views need broadening is the geographic expansion of trade perspectives. Traditionally, Canada has traded to the south with the United States or to the east with the United Kingdom or with Europe. U.S. trade dominates Canadian commercial ties. Dependence on the United States makes Canada extremely vulnerable both to fluctuations in the U.S. economy and to political and institutional changes in the U.S. that affect its trading relations. The MacDonald Royal Commission proposals notwithstanding, greater reliance on the U.S. is very risky. British and European trade is much less significant today and also likely to grow much more slowly, given the inward view of the European Economic Community. Thus, traditional trade patterns are fraught with difficulties.

However, looking West opens new trade vistas. Canada has some very significant advantages in the Pacific Rim markets, advantages not even enjoyed by the United States or other prospective trading partners in the region. First, Canada (via Vancouver and Prince Rupert) is closer to the Pacific Rim countries than is either the U.S. or Europe. Of the major developed nations, only Japan enjoys greater proximity. Second, Canada has an exceptionally fine image in the region. In China, for example, the memory of Norman Bethune, though overused, is very much alive and an element in future trade relations. So is Canada's early recognition of the People's Republic of China and the sponsorship by Canada of the PRC into the United Nations. Chinese memories are legendarily long and accurate. The absence of bad memories with respect to Canada, and the presence of many good ones, is a great plus.

Similarly, in Hong Kong the heroic stand of Canadian troops in defence of the island against the Japanese is still remembered. More recently, the estimated 60,000 Canadian university alumni from Hong Kong provide exceptional commercial and cultural ties with that city. The extent to which Canadian taxpayers subsidize university education is appreciated, as is the fact that Canadians made education accessible to the masses of Hong Kong people who could not otherwise afford such schooling. In Singapore and Malaysia, Canada's role through the Colombo Plan is still remembered. Moreover, Canadian membership in the British Commonwealth provides additional ties not enjoyed by either the United States, the EEC countries, except, of course, the U.K., or Japan.

To summarize, for a range of reasons in different countries, Canada has some very distinct and definite trading opportunities and advantages. Geographic proximity, past cultural and economic ties, and a generally favourable impression of Canada as a non-player in world geopolitical games, all combine to present Canada with major advantages in opening and expanding trading ties with the countries of the region.

Seen in this kind of context, Canada has exceptional scope to expand its trade both by increasing the range of goods and services that are traded and by increasing the range of countries traded with, in particular with Pacific

Rim countries. Additionally, countries like China, Malaysia, and Indonesia are eager to explore for resources and to extract and market them on world markets. Canada's significant knowledge base in these areas and its already strong relations with these countries suggest that great gains can be made and that policies need to be put in place to move vigorously into these markets. The Canadian edge in the region is real. However, it will not last indefinitely, and failure to act energetically and soon could seriously injure Canadian chances to take maximal advantage of the current and likely future opportunities that do and will likely continue to abound in the Pacific Rim region into the foreseeable future.

SOME SECTORAL PERSPECTIVES AND POLICY SUGGESTIONS

That Canada has major strengths in a number of areas beside the resource industries that have dominated trade in the past has already been touched on above. Here are some of the more obvious, as well as some not so obvious, sectors which can provide Canada with major options for greatly expanded trade.

A. Transportation and Communication

Canada's geographic scale and sparseness of population have combined to create unique needs for transportation and communication innovation. It is not surprising, therefore, to see Canada as a world leader in these fields. In the transportation of bulk commodities by rail and in shipping them by port and by sea, Canada has long been at the forefront of technological change. In the long-range transmission of gas and petroleum by pipeline, Canada is similarly among the most advanced nations in the world. Canada is also recognized as a standard-bearer in electricity transmission, particularly over long distances and rugged terrains, as it is in the development of small aircraft for operating over long distances in remote areas. In urban transportation, too, Canada is among the most sophisticated countries in the world. The Toronto Transit Commission is seen as one of the world's most successful transit operators and both Bombardier of Montreal and Urban Transportation Development Corporation of Toronto/Kingston are in the vanguard of technological innovation in the field.

In communication, Canada enjoys great respect because of its telecommunication satellite systems and radio and television services for remote areas. Canada's telephone system is among the most advanced anywhere, and Canadian cable television systems and their Canadian developed technologies can be favourably compared with the most sophisticated on earth. Canada is also at the forefront of communications software development with such systems as TELIDON and its extensions.

Canadian achievements in the areas of transportation and communication are impressive and provide the basis for major inroads in world trade both with respect to hardware and software and in the management systems that go with them. Countries like China are obvious and enormous potential markets for both transportation and communication know-how, while the dense cities of the Pacific Rim countries are obvious targets for urban transportation systems and operating know-how. Extension of this reasoning to other countries in the region, such as Australia and Indonesia, is straightforward.

Policy Discussion. Government has already been instrumental in the development of much of the advanced hardware and software in transportation and communication. Telecommunications satellites, the Dash-7 and Dash-8, bulk materials handling equipment at such ports as Roberts Bank and Ridley Island in British Columbia and urban transportation technologies of Ontario's UTDC all represent significant government accomplishments. Continuation of such government initiatives is clearly called for, as is the encouragement of research and development in these fields through both direct cash grants or through tax subsidies and accelerated write-offs. Sponsorship of demonstration projects as has been done with ALRT in Vancouver is another fruitful approach to bring the R & D ideas of the laboratory to fruition. The Transportation Development Agency and the federal Department of Communications, along with the National Research Council, have been most successful innovators in the field as have such crown corporations as CN Rail and Air Canada.

These past successful approaches should be continued and extended. New approaches should be considered as well via programme areas not usually associated with trade development at all. For example, the federal government spends billions annually on the Established Programmes Financing Act (EPFA) and through it on higher education and health care all across Canada. Clearly, such education expenditures give the federal government great leverage in directing educational dollars toward productive ends. In the present context, the direct earmarking of funds for engineering and basic sciences to develop new transportation and communication technologies is one alternative. Similarly, designating funds for training of transportation and communication managers and doing research on transportation and communication enterprises should be considered. So might scholarships and research stipends to encourage students and faculty to work in these areas where Canada already has a most significant world presence. More aggressive sponsorship of trade missions abroad, and even within Canada itself, are also called for to bring Canadian technologies to market in Canada and abroad. Closer cooperation with the provinces would assist on all of these policy initiatives.

B. *Finance, Insurance and Real Estate*

These service activities have been particularly well developed in Canada to the extent that some of the largest banking, insurance, and real estate companies in the world are Canadian. Moreover, the ability of Canadian companies in these fields to compete abroad is well known. Canadian banks have established themselves in the U.S., in Europe, and increasingly in the Pacific Rim region of concern here. Their success in these regions in international finance is well documented. More recently, Canadian brokerage firms have opened in China and elsewhere in Asia. Canadian insurance companies have had similar, if not as high profile, results. Finally, Canadian real estate development companies have made exceptional inroads into such competitive and sophisticated real estate markets as New York, Los Angeles, Houston, Dallas, and San Francisco. The ability of these three sectors to perform in highly competitive international environments augurs well for future growth and for envisioning these sectors as important elements in a broader approach to international trade. Lastly, Canadian stock exchanges are becoming recognized as leading sources of capital. In particular, the Vancouver Stock Exchange is emerging as one of the premier venture capital risk markets anywhere. All of this suggests that Canada is in an excellent position to take advantage of the NIDL and to promote its capital markets and investment services aggressively. The existence of potential global cities in Vancouver, Toronto, and Montreal provides the means for implementing such a financial services view anchored in one or more Canadian world cities.

However, the competition for being ranked as a global city is rough and getting rougher. Australia, for instance, has recently relaxed its overseas banking rules to allow more foreign banks to do business there and to get a piece of the Hong Kong/Singapore "action." Attracting the overseas Chinese is an important concomitant of policies to achieve global or world status. Current initiatives by the government of British Columbia to establish an international financial centre in Vancouver are very much in keeping with the thrust of this policy element. Japan's more flexible stance concerning offshore banks puts Tokyo squarely in the picture (Logan and Daly, 1984; *Far Eastern Economic Review*, 1 November 1984).

In short, the stakes are high, and competition is already quite heated, none of which is to say Canada, and particularly British Columbia, should flee from the fray. Rather, the experience of others provides Canada with outstanding information about which sorts of policies are needed to succeed, as well as about those policies that failed and why. One thing is clear, to propel Vancouver, Montreal, or Toronto into the rank of world or global cities will take a coordinated and considerable effort on the part of the federal, provincial, and municipal governments working in concert to achieve success.

Policy Discussion. The revision of the *Bank Act* that allowed increased foreign banking activity in Canada was an important step in opening up world banking markets to highly competitive Canadian banks. In addition, any expansion of merchandise and service trade is likely to have significant benefits for the banking and insurance sectors since these financial services provide key ingredients in all international trade and should be closely integrated into an expanded trade policy. Use of the Established Programmes Financing Act (EPFA) to stimulate management education in the areas of finance, insurance, and real estate deserves closer scrutiny. Greater research funding in these areas and perhaps graduate fellowship support would also enhance Canadian competitiveness in these areas. Rethinking of immigration and work permits is also needed to allow Canadian cities to attract international calibre entrepreneurs and managers. More flexible and aggressive policies on international landing rights, particularly at Vancouver International Airport, would promote access to Canada and greatly enhance the position of finance, insurance, and real estate firms here. Also needed is a more liberal tax policy to allow offshore loans to be packaged in Canada without present tax penalties. All these policies would combine to make it far easier for Pacific Rim business people to do business across the Pacific as well as for their Canadian-based subsidiaries to attract business from the region. Unfortunately, port and airport policies are usually not seen as being anything other than related to ports and airports, yet both have very significant implications for the growth and competitiveness of financial and real estate services in Canada, particularly in the West. Similarly, education and tax policy are also typically viewed in isolation. A much more comprehensive approach is called for, one that integrates the activities of all relevant levels of government and all relevant agencies of each level.[8]

C. Business and Related Commercial Services

With the advent of greater trading ties comes the need for higher levels of business and commercial services including a whole array of consultants, marketing and advertising services, printing and publishing, translation, legal, accounting, and related services. Canada has made some significant advances in some of these areas already, in management consulting, accounting, and legal areas, for example. Much greater opportunities are likely to be forthcoming as trade expands. These so-called "producer services" are key elements in global city functioning and in the NIDL. Comments earlier about financial services are relevant here as well accordingly.

Policy Discussion. While lacking the kind of direct control it can exert over financial services, there is still an important role for the federal government in stimulating business services. The kinds of educational initiatives discussed previously would clearly help to promote the human capital required for sophisticated and competitive business and commercial services. So would the more aggressive application of Canadian wordprocessing and software technologies to international management services. Sponsorship of demonstration projects in the application of extant Canadian technology in this realm would help to give Canadian firms in the field a most useful competitive edge. Also needed are the flexible landing rights and immigration and tax policies noted above. Coordinated effort and a comprehensive view are essential as discused under financial and related services.

D. Tourism and Travel

Often touted as British Columbia's second leading industry (behind forest products), tourism and travel represents an extraordinary opportunity for Canada as a whole and the ten provinces separately for several reasons. First, tourism is an important earner of foreign exchange, and given Canada's diversity and scenic beauty, there clearly exist some significant natural comparative advantages. Second, clever promotion of tourism and travel *domestically* can help to create greater appreciation for the diversity that is Canada, greater understanding of Canada's hotly contested federal system, and perhaps even reduced foreign travel by Canadians with additional foreign exchange benefits. Third, luring people to Canada on pleasure cannot but help enormously in establishing commercial interest and laying the groundwork for possible future trading opportunities. Fourth, properly promoted and developed travel and tourism programmes can significantly add to the enjoyment of business travellers, encourage longer stays, and the accompaniment of families, all leading to higher tourist spending. Heightened enjoyment and greater knowledge about Canada has obvious future benefits for increased levels of trading activity as well.

Policy Discussion. Tourism is a service industry, so many of the points made about other service industries apply here as well. Most notably, denser airline ties with other nations, especially those in Asia, hold the prospect for expanding tourist links and with them business ties. Better education and training for tourism and travel personnel are also needed. Federal dollars could make a large difference. However, the most important element is probably vigorous, effective promotion and marketing of Canada as a tourist destination. Much more aggressive marketing is needed here. In particular, federal efforts need to be closely coordinated with provincial and even local tourist promotion efforts to maximize the effectiveness of campaigns. The use of international expositions such as the upcoming EXPO '86 in Vancouver also has considerable potential as does the development of such internationally known regional activities as the Calgary Stampede, Edmonton's Klondike Days, Vancouver's Sea Festival, and Quebec City's Carneval. An integral part of the promotion activity should be federal support for tourist activities either through direct federal spending or co-spending with provinces or through tax expenditures and credits for firms making major contributions to the tourism and travel industry. The recent Cathay Pacific (a Hong Kong-based company) blitz across Asia advertising Vancouver as the gateway to North America is a case in point, and similar efforts should receive great moral and even financial support from the federal and provincial governments. Canadian tourism and travel firms should be strongly encouraged to demonstrate comparable initiative on their own. The benefits are potentially enormous, both directly from tourism and tourist spending and from the indirect trade possibilities that can derive from greater numbers of business people vacationing in Canada.

E. Educational Services

Canadian institutions of higher learning are widely respected and represent another heretofore ignored element of an expanded trade policy. These institutions have a number of potential contributions to make. First, these institutions are needed to provide the human capital for expanded trade in areas such as finance, insurance, and real estate and transportation and communication. Second, they provide an exceptional opportunity to educate the coming generations of managers and decision-makers from abroad, particularly from the Pacific Rim region because of the paucity of universities and regional colleges there. Educating future leaders of the region not only helps to familiarize these people with Canada: more importantly, it also familiarizes them with Canada's next generation of leaders. Third, particularly for children of current business and government leaders, having their children in Canada creates a current bond between Canada and the parents. Visits to the children are also visits to Canada and provide information about Canada with the resulting trade potential cited earlier. Fourth, and last, opening up Canadian post-secondary institutions yields enormous goodwill and an extremely favourable disposition to look to Canada in future for business, cultural, and intergovernmental dealings. The review of the overseas Chinese and the role of education in their investment and business decisions reinforces and gives empirical support to this point. A coordinated education focus is a must as well for that elusive and much pursued "global" city label.

Policy Discussion. The government of Canada has significant leverage in the post-secondary education area through the Established Programmes Financing Act (EPFA). This act could provide one vehicle for encouraging off-shore students to study in Canadian post-secondary institutions. Earmarking portions of the funding for off-shore students would be an obvious approach. The government of Canada could alternatively provide monies abroad for scholarships and bursaries or provide direct subsidies to Canadian institutions through existing agencies such as the Canadian International Development Agency (CIDA). There is great precedent for such an approach. Two decades ago CIDA, through the Colombo Plan, was instrumental in establishing business schools in both Kuala Lumpur and Singapore. Most recently, CIDA has embarked on a large-scale project of educational aid to the People's Republic of China. These programmes could be expanded to other countries in the region, while at the same time open scholarship competitions could be developed. Another variant would see scholarships apportioned to Canadian embassies and high commissions in the region for direct award by these arms of the government of Canada in the Pacific Rim region. In either case, some mixture of merit and need should be sought in the selection criteria, since those who can pay should contribute according to their ability for educational services, while those who cannot should not be denied access to Canadian educational institutions.

Another approach could see the government of Canada stimulating research in and about the Pacific Rim region. This model would bring Canadian researchers and educators to the region for study and encourage the development of research materials and libraries in Canada, all aimed at increasing Canadian knowledge of the region and its people and indirectly providing knowledge about Canadian opportunities and potential there. The government of Canada could also encourage Canadian enterprises to send their employees back to school, such employees could include both nationals of Pacific Rim countries and Canadians. Generous tax credits or cost-sharing programmes with these Canadian enterprises could help to achieve these results. Without professionals who are knowledgeable about regional cultures, establishing firm and enduring footholds around the Pacific Rim will be a random and difficult process.

So far the role of the federal government has been the focus. However, education is a provincial matter, and the provincial governments need to be included and worked with closely in any of the schemes suggested above. The federal government can (and should) take the lead, but it should also encourage partnership with each of the provinces who stand to reap most of the benefits outlined here. There is one area where the provincial governments need to act directly, and the need is great indeed. This relates to so-called "visa schools." These schools are infamous in Southeast Asia, especially for their often misleading advertising and also for their frequently fraudulent behaviour of taking fees in advance and often closing their doors before the end of the school year. Provincial governments should license *all* such schools and/or provide similar educational services at the secondary school level (for full cost recovery or on a subsidized basis) by using public secondary schools. Failure to do so quickly is likely to tarnish greatly an otherwise excellent Canadian image. The federal government can exert considerable pressure here as well on the provinces. It can also seek out information about fraudulent visa schools and/or about fully accredited visa schools and only provide information or student visas (in the extreme case) to legitimate operations. However, action should be taken speedily since this is a festering sore and could undo much of the good that could be derived from the suggestions of this section. This is a particularly important area for action with respect to the overseas Chinese in light of their enormous stress on education, and it is they who have suffered most at the hands of unethical private schools to date.

One last point, education is another urban-centred activity which complements the financial services option noted above as well as the health care policy to be set out below. More fundamentally, it further reinforces the global city idea and provides a means for Canada to tap into that vital growing world city network in a coherent fashion by focussing these policies on cities to provide the infrastructure for one or more Canadian global cities.

F. Health and Health Technology

Even before the current surplus physician "crisis" in Canada there, was excellent reason to view Canadian health care system and its supporting technology as a marvelous "export" option. In the Pacific Rim, outside of Japan and possibly Singapore once it completes its huge new medical school, the quality and availability of medical services is poor. People in the region, especially the wealthy, almost never use health care facilities there except on an emergency basis. The United States (Hawaii and California) and the United Kingdom have been preferred locations for receiving health care. Canada, it would seem, is in an excellent position to move into the Pacific Rim health care market. Proximity through Vancouver to the region is great as is the availability of world class health care in Canada. Recent moves to expand the University of British Columbia medical school, surpluses of physicians from Alberta's two medical schools, and growing interest in medical high technology and research all provide the background against which aggressive promotion of health care to residents of the Pacific Rim can be viewed. In passing, it should be noted that Rochester, Minnesota, has been "exporting" health services for decades (and quite profitably too) via the Mayo clinic, and there is no reason why Canada cannot market Canadian health care services similarly. As with education, health care provides a means to attract people to Canada and open the way to broader business dealings.

Policy Discussion. Federal leverage here is great once again despite the fact that health delivery is essentially a provincial and local function. The federal government through the EPFA exerts major influence on the health care system in Canada, and it could use this influence to "encourage" provinces to energetically export and market abroad their health services. Tying EPFA funds, or supplementary R & D funds for health care technologies, to requirements that provinces begin marketing a certain percentage of health care abroad in the Pacific Rim region could be effective. The provinces could easily pursue such policies independently also. Using Canadian embassies, high commissions, and consulates to help market these services would assist the provinces and could be part of the federal/provincial partnership to promote these services abroad. Encouraging R & D in health care technologies (including management as a health care technology) should be done in parallel through EPFA university funding, through the National Science and Engineering Research Council (NSERC) and Medical Sciences Research Council (MSRC), through the Social Sciences and Humanities Research Council of Canada (SSHRCC) (to study the economic and social aspects of health care), and through standard tax credits and write-offs. This programme should be coordinated with airlines especially and with tourist and travel services to provide for the family of the patient as well as for the patient upon recovery.

G. Resource Extraction and Resource Extracting Technology and Services

At the start of this policy section, it was suggested that it is important to view traditional Canadian natural resource and semi-finished manufactures in a different light as embodying both the resource itself (the traditional "hewers and drawers" approach) and the technological know-how to extract, transport, finance, and manage the resource extraction and marketing process as a whole.

Coal was used in the earlier example, but lumber and forest products could have served equally well. The essential point to be made here is that Canada does in fact sell more than the resources themselves. Canadian resources are backed up by exceptional transportation technology and know-how, by a consulting engineering industry of world class proportions and skill, by international financiers and marketers, by excellent universities providing the human capital to maintain the edge, and by governments promoting growth in trade and technology. In the case of coal, for instance, the federal government has provided the University of British Columbia with a first-rate facility in the form of the Coal Research Institute. Similar federal support of the forest industry in British Columbia through FORINTEK and FORIC provide the wherewithal by which Canada can continue to develop pioneering technologies and approaches to resource extraction and resource marketing abroad. More needs to be done and to be done in a coordinated fashion jointly with the provinces and with the private sector.

However, a fundamental shift in perspective is needed here too. These technological support services should not be seen as being mere inputs to the production and marketing of resources. Rather they need to be seen as being highly valued and readily marketed *in their own right.* Accordingly, the markets for these technologies and management systems need to be pursued *in parallel* with the marketing of the resources themselves. Competition is fierce and growing in the natural resource world marketplace. Through an aggressive marketing programme for Canadian resource-oriented technologies, what is lost in resource contracts can more than be made up for in high value added resource extraction consulting and equipment sales. These markets can be straddled as a result, broadening the Canadian export base and reducing some of the uncertainty that derives from competing in these world markets.

Policy Discussion. While it is not responsible for natural resources, the federal government does have exceptional influence in this area. It can promote additional facilities such as the FORINTEK and Coal Research Centre activities. It can provide direct research grants to universities and private sector resource companies. It can also provide generous tax write-offs and subsidies for R & D in the area. It can offer scholarships and bursaries to students to develop future human capital. Embassies, high commissions, and consulates can be used once again to promote this service-technology approach to resources in a world setting. Crown corporations like CN Rail, long a world leader in moving bulk materials, can be viewed as exporters of their expertise. So can bulk materials handlers at the large ports. Similar opportunities exist in the agricultural sector where the Canadian government exerts great power and where Canada can be seen to be exporting agricultural technology and knowledge as much as wheat. What is required for all of these scenarios is a realization on the part of the federal government that technology/knowledge exports are already embodied in our resource exports and that they can be sold in a disembodied form directly through proper promotion, R & D, and marketing. The provincial governments have a completely analogous and parallel role and can use their own crown corporations and taxing powers to similar advantage.

H. Retired Entrepreneurs, Engineers, and Managers

With the aging of the Canadian population there exists a looming social problem. However, just as growing competition in world resource markets created an opportunity for the marketing of knowledge and technology, so does the changing age structure of Canada's population provide significant export opportunities, if viewed appropriately.

Retired entrepreneurs represent a significant opportunity to make use of the enormous human capital that these people have acquired during their working years. CIDA has used such people in the past to assist developing nations. Much greater use still could be made as their numbers grow, and with this increase in number grows the body of knowledge these people represent.

Canada's programme of allowing retired entrepreneurs from abroad to settle in Canada under certain well-specified conditions is also worthy of expansion. This programme allows Canada to tap foreign entrepreneurial expertise and connections. As such, it is particularly attractive to people from Southeast Asian countries and therefore fits in directly with the discussion in this book. Taking both sets of entrepreneurs together provides Canada with a potentially significant resource, this time human, that can yield significant trade possibilities. These resources can and should be mobilized for expanded trading opportunities.

Policy Discussion. Through the Canada Pension Plan and other social assistance schemes, governments are already very much involved with Canadian retirees. Through immigration policy, the government of Canada is similarly involved with immigrant retirees. Greater emphasis should be placed on making use of these resources. With respect to Canadian nationals, innovative schooling and degree courses should be pursued with federal initiatives to assist retired people to maintain the level of their human capital. Registers of retired experts should be established and should be used for staffing overseas activities and initiating new ventures that draw on foreign experience. Retirees should have available to them scholarships for degree and non-degree courses and in particular for language training. They have the time to acquire such skills, which are essential in future trading ventures. Finally, the foreign retired entrepreneur programmes should be expanded and more effort directed toward attracting such people to Canada. Their know-how, connections, and energy are an exceptional resource base for broadening the Canadian economy and expanding its trade linkages. Again, the discussion of overseas Chinese highlighted the importance of the connections and the trust they embody.

Summing Up

In this policy discussion, issues have been raised that go well beyond the question of overseas Chinese real estate investment or the Pacific Rim. Instead, the scope of the argument has been opened up to consider a full range of ideas directed at expanding perceptions of possible future trade activites for Canada. These ideas and the resulting discussion has been focussed on the Pacific Rim since this region provides the most exciting potential for the future and builds nicely on the primary focus of this volume, the real estate investment behaviour of the overseas Chinese. A variety of sectors have been discussed, many of which have not been seen traditionally as trade-related in the past (such as health care), but which in fact have significant roles to play in an expanded world view. Numerous policies have been delineated, usually from the federal vantage point, that could be used effectively to help bring about changed trade patterns that take advantage of the changes currently underway in the larger world economy (NIDL), and particularly in its cities. This global city element is particularly important as it provides Canada with the means to get "plugged" into the emerging world economy at a very high level.

CAPITULATION AND RETURN TO OVERSEAS CHINESE URBAN
REAL ESTATE INVESTMENTS

Major changes are currently wrenching the world economy out of the relative comfort and stability of the past two decades. Three changes are worth restating. First, there has been a shift away from producing goods and processing materials toward the production and processing of information and services. The impacts on cities have been particularly profound and are unlikely to abate in the coming decade (Stanback and Noyelle, 1982; Kwok, 1982; Jacobs, 1984a and 1984b). Out of these changes have emerged a number of cities that thrive on information generation and processing and that have risen to the forefront of the emerging new economic structure, relegating goods and materials producers to a much weaker secondary position (Cohen, 1981, Frobel, Heinrichs, and Kreye, 1980). Financial transactions and expertise in moving capital internationally are of particular importance in the evolution of the changing system of world cities (McGee, 1984; Thrift, 1983). Looking into the future and the effects of "the new international division of labor" and the related structural changes discussed above, Cohen suggests:

These trends, since they place more pressure on corporations and financial institutions in developed nations, will probably tend to further concentrate corporate and financial decision-making in present world centers, drawing decision-making activities away from national or regional centers. (1981:310-11)

It is as if this highly articulated system, of cities most notably, obviates much national economic policy, since so many basic economic decisions reside in global corporations in global cities. Summarizing the impacts of this emerging system of world cities and its ties to international capital markets and to national and regional economic development policy, Daly concludes:

The forging of a global economy, therefore, has linked individual nations in a fashion never before seen within the capitalist era. Global manufacturing, global marketing and global financing characterize the system, and within it the freedom of individual nations to frame national or regional policies of development has been greatly reduced. The new system renders obsolete much of the previous theorizing about regional development. (1984:1019)

The third change of relevance to present discussions is the emergence of the Pacific Rim as a major economic region. Moreover, its extraordinary growth rate is likely to propel it further up into the first rank of economic actors on the world scene. Gazing into the future in their study of the Eastasia region, Hofheinz and Calder assert:

But it is one thing to doubt whether Eastasia can continue to grow at the same phenomenal rate, and quite another to believe that its fortunes will be reversed. Short of a world war or some other cataclysmic event that interrupts the flow of commerce and raw materials, it is hard to conceive of a dramatic decline in Eastasian growth and performance, and the possibility exists of a considerable and sustained upward thrust. Given the deep-seated ills of Western societies, Eastasia may gain against the West even if, in comparison with past performance; it only stands still. (1982:251)

These three elements interact strongly and hold special meaning for the subject of interest here, overseas Chinese real estate around the Pacific Rim. To begin, as the world moves toward information-based economies strongly rooted in both information networks and in advanced professional skills for generating and analysing information, Chinese enterprises and families should share disproportionately in this movement in view of their extensive international commercial ties and their past and continued heavy emphasis on education, particularly in the professions. Second, the growing importance of international finance (Logan and Daly, 1984) and its increasing focus on "world cities" (Thrift, 1983:2-9) again imply an expanded role for overseas Chinese in the development of world cities and the associated world financial dealings. Their traditional skills and experience with money (Freedman, 1979:23-26) and in international and regional banking (Wu and Wu, 1980:96-101; Wu (1983:115-16) place the Chinese in an ideal position to take advantage of the kinds of changes that have been discussed here relating to the world economic and urban orders. Third, the expected continued growth of the Eastasia region and the surplus capital such growth is likely to produce suggest that there will be in future considerable additional sources of capital for international investment, and there is no reason to believe that real estate will not continue to be a major use of those funds. Fourth and finally, the continued ascendancy of a relatively limited number of key urban areas around the world implies that much of the international real estate investment of the future will be directed toward these centres. Here again, existing Chinese populations in these cities, the presence of world class educational institutions, and access to Asia by air from all of them suggest that the Nanyang Chinese will continue to seek sound real estate investment in such world cities and in smaller cities that are moving into world class status (Thrift, 1983:10-15). Moreover, given the location of these cities overwhelmingly in English-speaking and stable democracies (Canada, the U.S., the U.K., and Australia), the findings of the present study and the issues that it raises should become increasingly important over time.

In summary, the present study began with modest goals and focus. It has become apparent, however, in the course of completing this research that largely by accident, the study has stumbled upon an area that is of great significance already in world economic affairs and, much more to the point, one that is likely to increase substantially in significance over the coming decade or so. The complexity which has been seen to characterize overseas Chinese societies, business practices, family relations, educational objectives and the need to operate in a frequently hostile and always uncertain world demand further unravelling, analysis, and answers. The present effort is a tentative start in the direction of greater understanding. As the great classical sage Lao Tzu observed, "the journey of a thousand li begins with a single step."

Notes

1. One issue that has been carefully avoided is that of precisely defining the overseas Chinese. The authoritative study by Purcell (1965) is equally circumspect. Similarly, Williams deals with the issue with the following broad definition to which we subscribe:

   An overseas Chinese is a person of some Chinese ancestry who views residence abroad as compatible with Chinese cultural identity and less certainly with some remote Chinese political orientation. The overseas Chinese considers his expatriation the result of his own or his forebears' economic strivings. He regards himself as a member of the overseas Chinese people, which is in turn, part of the greater Chinese nation, and is so regarded by those around him. (Williams, 1966:6)

2. Results that are consistent with and complement those presented by Wu can be found in most of the other volumes cited earlier that deal with overseas Chinese business culture and values. Specifically, see: Ward, 1972; Silin, 1972; De Glopper, 1972; Omohundro, 1973 and 1981; Freedman, 1979; Hicks and Redding, 1983; Olsen, 1972; Purcell, 1965; and Williams, 1966. Family, kinship and trust also permeate virtually every paper in Volume 1 of Lim and Gosling, 1983, where ethnic Chinese economic activity in Southeast Asia is the focus.

3. Here apologies are made to the late Richard Hughes (1968) for borrowing from the title to his classic analysis of Hong Kong's political conundrum, *Hong Kong: Borrowed Place, Borrowed Time*.

4. For example, the two universities in Hong Kong, Hong Kong University and the Chinese University of Hong Kong at Shatin, have a combined enrolment of roughly 11,000 students to service a highly education conscious and education seeking population of roughly 5.5 million people. In contrast, the province of British Columbia has three universities with combined full-time enrolments in excess of 40,000 students to service 2.4 million not-so-educationally oriented people.

5. Malyasian Islamic fundamentalism is of considerable concern to the Malaysian Chinese. See *Asiaweek*, 24 August 1984 (pp. 22-31), 14 September 1984 (pp. 23-27), and 23 November 1984, (pp. 11-17). Also see Clad, 1984, in the *Far Eastern Economic Review*, 18 October 1984.

6. Discrimination against the overseas Chinese continues in many places but perhaps most notably and significantly in Malaysia and Indonesia (Coppel, 1982). Recent bombings in Jakarta's Chinatown and against Chinese businesses highlight the fact that resentment against the ethnic Chinese is far from passing from the scene (Awanohara, 1984). In Malaysia, this combines with Islamic fundamentalism to make the position of the Chinese uncertain (Clad, 1984; *Asiaweek*, 24 August and 14 September 1984).

7. The changing environment of Australian banks as Australia strives for the "global city connection" is outlined in McDonald, 1984, in the *Far Eastern Economic Review*.

8. Some interesting attempts at such coordinated policy are forthcoming. The MacDonald Royal Commission is clearly taking a broad, comprehensive, and integrated view aimed at development of coordinated policies. The City of Vancouver Economic Advisory Commission has developed a detailed economic strategy for the City and the region which sees "invisible" exports as being key elements in the future economy of the area and also sees the Pacific Rim as the major market for such exports. Finally, the Province of British Columbia is in the process of developing a set of strategies to create a major International Financial Centre in Vancouver to tap into the global city network and all that has been discussed above. In each instance, the realization that no one level of government can perform the job adequately is explicit, as is the very crucial role to be played by the private sector in "making it all happen" given the right conditions by coordinated government actions.

APPENDIX TABLE 1
POPULATION

	Census (yr.)	1980*	1985*
Australia	13,548,472 (1976)	14,480,000	15,599,000
Canada	24,274,000 (1981)	24,070,000	25,827,000
China	1,056,000,000 (1982)	975,000,000	992,200,000
Hong Kong	3,948,179 (1971)†	4,801,000	—
Indonesia	119,291,290 (1971)	147,490,298[1]	176,735,000
Japan	111,933,818 (1975)	118,747,000	126,669,000
Malaysia	10,413,524 (1970)	13,790,000	15,909,000
New Zealand	3,129,383 (1976)	3,167,400[2]	3,674,000
Philippines	41,831,045 (1975)	50,119,000	57,820,000
Singapore	2,127,031 (1970)	2,427,000	2,628,000
South Korea	34,688,000 (1975)	40,457,000	45,107,000
Taiwan	13,161,023 (1966)	17,696,000	19,538,000
Thailand	34,152,000 (1970)	47,670,000	55,646,000[3]
United States	231,106,727 (1980)	231,106,727	238,648,000

*Figures are estimated unless otherwise noted.

[1]1980 census.
[2]1981 census.
[3]1984 estimate.

Sources: Collier's Encyclopedia, 1982.
World Book Encyclopedia, 1980.
†Statistical Yearbook, 1981.

APPENDIX TABLE 2
GROSS DOMESTIC PRODUCT
($US millions)
1960-1982

	1960	1982	%Change
Australia	16,370	164,210	11.049
Canada	39,930	289,570	9.424
China	42,770*	260,400	8.557
Hong Kong	950	24,440	15.907
Indonesia	8,670	90,160	11.231
Japan	44,000	1,061,920	15.571
Malaysia	2,290	25,870	11.651
New Zealand	3,940	23,820	8.523
Philippines	6,960	39,850	8.255
Singapore	700	14,650	14.824
South Korea	3,810	68,420	14.028
Thailand	2,550	36,790	12.899
United States	505,300	3,009,600	8.449

*1961 figure.

Source: World Development Report, 1984, pp. 222-23.

APPENDIX TABLE 3
GNP PER CAPITA
($US)

	1982 Dollars	Average Annual Growth 1960-1982(%)
Australia	11,140	2.4
Canada	11,320	3.1
China	310	5.0
Hong Kong	5,340	7.0
Indonesia	580	4.2
Japan	10,080	6.1
Malaysia	1,860	4.3
New Zealand	7,920	1.5
Philippines	820	2.8
Singapore	5,910	7.4
South Korea	1,910	6.6
Thailand	790	4.5
United States	13,160	2.2

Source: World Development Report, 1984, pp. 218-19.

APPENDIX TABLE 4

PRIVATE CONSUMPTION
GROSS DOMESTIC INVESTMENT
Average Annual Growth Rate (%)
1970-1982

	Private Consumption	Gross Domestic Investment
Australia	2.7	1.1
Canada	3.9	3.3
China	5.1	6.4
Hong Kong	10.0	13.6
Indonesia	9.0	13.7
Japan	4.1	3.3
Malaysia	7.2	11.4
New Zealand	1.5	-0.1
Philippines	4.9	9.3
Singapore	6.2	8.7
South Korea	6.8	11.0
Thailand	6.1	6.4
United States	3.4	1.3

Source: World Development Report, 1984, pp. 224-25.

APPENDIX TABLE 5
ASIA AND THE PACIFIC: EXPORTS (fob) 1976-1981
($US millions)

Countries	1976	% of Total*	1977	% of Total*	1978	% of Total*	1979	% of Total*	1980	% of Total*	1981	% of Total*
Australia	13,149	4.7	13,359	4.3	14,417	3.9	18,687	4.2	22,094	4.1	21,762	3.7
Canada†	38,957	14.0	41,876	13.5	46,567	12.7	56,053	12.6	65,123	11.9	69,907	11.8
Hong Kong	8,526	3.1	9,626	3.1	11,499	3.1	15,151	3.4	19,720	3.6	21,738	3.7
Indonesia	8,546	3.1	10,853	3.5	11,643	3.2	15,590	3.5	21,909	4.0	22,260	3.8
Japan	67,320	24.2	81,084	26.1	98,338	26.8	103,093	23.3	130,560	24.0	152,011	25.7
Malaysia†	3,955	1.4	4,565	1.5	5,937	1.6	8,710	2.0	10,439	1.9	9,032	1.5
New Zealand	2,798	1.0	3,195	1.0	3,739	1.0	4,699	1.1	5,407	1.0	5,607	0.9
Philippines	2,574	0.9	3,151	1.0	3,425	0.9	4,576	1.0	5,710	1.0	5,757	1.0
Singapore	6,585	2.4	8,241	2.7	10,134	2.8	14,233	3.2	19,376	3.6	20,968	3.5
South Korea	7,715	2.8	10,046	3.2	12,711	3.5	15,055	3.4	17,505	3.2	21,254	3.6
Thailand	2,980	1.1	3,482	1.1	4,075	1.1	5,298	1.2	6,505	1.2	6,784	1.1
United States†	115,340	41.4	121,212	39.0	143,766	39.3	182,025	41.1	220,786	40.5	233,739	39.6
TOTAL	278,445	100.0	310,690	100.0	366,251	100.0	443,170	100.0	545,134	100.0	590,819	100.0

*Total may not equal 100.0 owing to rounding.

Source: Statistical Yearbook for Asia and the Pacific, 1981.
United Nations.
†Statistical Yearbook, 1981, United Nations.

APPENDIX TABLE 6

ASIA AND THE PACIFIC: IMPORTS (cif) 1976-1981

($US millions)

Countries	1976	% of Total*	1977	% of Total*	1978	% of Total*	1979	% of Total*	1980	% of Total*	1981	% of Total*
Australia	11,162	3.8	12,257	3.7	14,122	3.6	18,228	3.7	20,255	3.4	23,758	3.8
Canada†	37,991	13.1	39,808	11.9	43,868	11.2	53,685	10.9	59,227	10.0	66,010	10.4
Hong Kong	8,882	3.1	10,457	3.1	13,452	3.4	17,138	3.5	22,397	3.8	23,994	3.8
Indonesia	5,673	2.0	6,230	1.9	6,690	1.7	7,202	1.5	10,834	1.8	13,272	2.1
Japan	64,891	22.3	71,325	21.3	79,900	20.4	110,670	22.5	140,648	23.9	143,257	22.6
Malaysia†	3,352	1.2	4,020	1.2	5,265	1.3	7,030	1.4	9,675	1.6	10,234	1.6
New Zealand	3,255	1.1	3,361	1.0	3,489	0.9	4,553	0.9	5,472	0.9	5,739	0.9
Philippines	3,952	1.4	4,270	1.3	5,059	1.3	6,563	1.3	8,185	1.4	8,864	1.4
Singapore	9,070	3.1	10,471	3.1	13,049	3.3	17,635	3.6	24,002	4.1	27,571	4.4
South Korea	8,774	3.0	10,810	3.2	14,972	3.8	20,339	4.1	22,292	3.8	26,131	4.1
Thailand	3,572	1.2	4,639	1.4	5,381	1.4	7,158	1.5	9,454	1.6	10,330	1.6
United States†	129,896	44.7	157,560	47.0	186,044	47.5	222,228	45.1	256,984	43.6	273,352	43.2
TOTAL	290,470	100.0	335,208	100.0	391,291	100.0	492,429	100.0	589,425	100.0	632,512	100.0

*Total may not equal 100.0 owing to rounding

Source: Statistical Yearbook for Asia and the Pacific, 1980.
  United Nations.
    †Statistical Yearbook, 1981, United Nations.

APPENDIX TABLE 7

DEPENDENCE ON TRADE* WITHIN THE PACIFIC BASIN AND OUTSIDE IT
(percentages)

			Trade with		
Countries	Japan	USA	Other Pacific region	Total Pacific Basin	Rest of world
Australia	22	17	16	55	45
Canada	5	67	4	76	24
Taiwan	22	31	18	71	29
Hong Kong	15	19	35	69	31
Indonesia	41	18	17	76	24
Japan	—	22	34	56	44
South Korea	28	25	11	64	36
Malaysia	24	16	34	74	26
New Zealand	14	14	31	59	41
Philippines	24	26	14	64	36
Singapore	14	14	32	60	40
Thailand	24	14	20	58	42
United States	11	—	34	45	55
China	26	10	4	40	60
North Korea	30	—	65	95	5

*Early 1980s.

Source: Kirby, 1983, p. 16

APPENDIX TABLE 8

INVISIBLE TRADE (Services, Transport, Banking, Tourism)
($US bn)

	Imports			Exports			Balance	
Countries	1974	1979	% Growth	1974	1979	% Growth	1974	1979
World	255	514	102	221	490	122	-34	-24
United States	37	70	90	46	105	127	9	35
Japan	18	35	93	12	24	100	-6	-9
Canada	10	17	70	6	8	32	-4	-9
Australia	5	7	53	2	3	36	-34	-24
Malaysia	1	3	220	0.4	1	210	-0.6	2
Singapore	1	2	113	2	4	85	-34	-24
Philippines	0.8	2	125	0.8	2	90	—	—
Chile	0.4	2	417	0.2	1	520	-0.2	-1
Peru	0.7	2	110	0.3	0.6	115	-0.4	-0.9
Total of above*	44	82	86	27	51	89	-17	-33

*Excluding USA.

N.B.: Totals may not add owing to rounding.

Source: Kirby, 1983, p. 23.

APPENDIX TABLE 9
CANADA: DOMESTIC EXPORTS BY COUNTRY
($CDN 000s)

	1979	% of Total	1980	% of Total	1981	% of Total	1982	% of Total	1983	% of Total	% Change			
											80/79	81/80	82/81	83/82
China	604,132	0.9	869,545	1.2	1,017,554	1.2	1,228,754	1.5	1,605,021	1.8	43.9	13.8	20.7	30.6
Hong Kong	137,621	0.2	192,875	0.3	184,219	0.2	242,744	0.3	221,157	0.3	40.1	-5.3	31.7	-8.9
Indonesia	62,643	0.1	215,029	0.3	94,088	0.1	201,537	0.2	209,844	0.2	243.2	-57.2	114.2	4.0
Japan	4,083,071	6.3	4,364,455	5.9	4,497,783	5.5	4,572,865	5.6	4,733,878	5.4	6.8	2.8	1.6	3.5
Malaysia	65,329	0.1	93,015	0.1	125,706	0.2	118,205	0.1	113,977	0.1	42.3	34.6	-6.1	-3.4
Philippines	84,870	0.1	108,212	0.1	83,096	0.1	102,487	0.1	77,168	0.1	27.5	-25.4	23.3	-24.7
Singapore	114,828	0.2	198,161	0.3	145,661	0.2	154,268	0.2	126,927	0.2	72.5	-26.5	5.9	-17.7
South Korea	365,412	0.6	504,332	0.7	444,828	0.6	488,429	0.6	554,962	0.6	38.0	-11.5	9.8	13.6
Taiwan	103,756	0.2	251,610	0.3	232,826	0.3	292,779	0.4	341,271	0.4	142.5	-7.0	25.7	16.5
Thailand	87,248	0.1	141,602	0.2	116,005	0.1	142,378	0.2	146,486	0.2	62.2	-19.2	22.7	2.8
Australia	557,922	0.9	664,308	0.9	777,104	0.9	650,679	0.8	438,425	0.5	19.0	16.4	-16.2	-32.6
New Zealand	90,796	0.1	112,657	0.2	139,863	0.2	156,936	0.2	122,129	0.1	24.0	22.3	12.2	-22.1
United States	43,519,100	67.7	46,827,635	63.1	53,899,776	66.3	55,839,675	68.2	64,460,595	72.9	7.6	14.6	3.5	15.4
EEC	7,250,088	11.3	9,519,105	12.8	8,802,550	10.8	7,371,830	9.0	7,629,844	8.6	31.3	-0.1	-16.3	3.5
Other	7,190,485	11.2	10,196,802	13.7	10,775,672	13.3	10,268,157	12.5	7,643,910	8.6	14.2	5.8	-4.7	-25.6
To all Countries	64,317,301	100.0	74,259,343	100.0	81,336,731	100.0	81,828,704	100.0	88,425,594	100.0	15.4	8.9	0.6	8.0

Source: Statistics Canada 65-001, December 1983, Tables X-1, X-2.

APPENDIX TABLE 10
CANADA: IMPORTS BY COUNTRY
($CDN 000s)

	1979	% of Total	1980	% of Total	1981	% of Total	1982	% of Total	1983	% of Total	% Change 80/79	81/80	82/81	83/82
China	167,451	0.3	155,087	0.2	220,013	0.3	203,654	0.3	254,864	0.3	-7.3	42.0	-7.4	20.7
Hong Kong	427,223	0.7	574,438	0.8	674,531	0.9	668,839	1.0	820,740	1.1	34.4	17.2	-0.8	22.7
Indonesia	42,108	0.1	28,913	0.0*	36,961	0.0	30,269	0.1	39,884	0.1	-31.3	27.8	-18.1	31.7
Japan	2,158,764	3.4	2,795,844	4.0	4,056,696	5.1	3,536,119	5.2	4,409,919	5.8	29.5	44.4	-12.8	24.7
Malaysia	96,284	0.2	83,389	0.1	99,979	0.1	89,193	0.1	115,587	0.2	-13.4	18.8	-10.7	29.5
Philippines	78,285	0.1	101,481	0.1	108,682	0.1	82,219	0.1	88,151	0.1	29.6	6.7	-24.3	7.2
Singapore	164,086	0.3	149,665	0.2	174,629	0.2	163,562	0.2	168,990	0.2	-8.7	16.9	-6.3	3.3
South Korea	462,864	0.7	414,382	0.6	608,172	0.8	586,447	0.9	791,369	1.0	-10.4	46.6	-3.5	34.9
Taiwan	522,065	0.8	557,589	0.8	729,142	0.9	661,268	1.0	925,875	1.2	6.8	30.7	-9.3	40.0
Thailand	31,705	0.1	24,688	0.0	33,067	0.0	33,785	0.0	60,467	0.1	-22.1	33.5	2.1	78.9
Australia	461,742	0.7	516,860	0.7	497,593	0.6	446,096	0.7	358,119	0.5	11.9	-3.9	-10.3	-19.7
New Zealand	135,088	0.2	146,950	0.2	145,740	0.2	140,455	0.2	156,570	0.2	8.7	-0.6	-3.6	11.4
United States	45,571,224	72.5	48,473,244	70.1	54,537,500	68.8	47,916,788	70.1	54,202,926	71.6	6.4	11.7	-12.1	13.1
EEC	5,618,933	8.9	5,576,540	8.1	6,501,671	8.0	5,708,405	8.4	5,951,219	7.9	1.0	13.7	-12.2	4.3
Other	6,932,883	11.0	9,528,589	13.8	11,157,339	13.8	7,659,013	11.2	7,358,610	9.7	37.4	14.1	-31.4	-3.9
To All Countries	62,870,705	100.0	69,127,659	100.0	79,481,715	100.0	67,926,112	100.0	75,694,290	100.0	9.9	13.7	-14.5	11.4

Source: Statistics Canada 65-001, December 1983, Tables M-1, M-2.

APPENDIX TABLE 11
IMPORTS AND EXPORTS

AUSTRALIA

Imports: plant and capital equipment, machinery, transportation equipment.

Exports: minerals (bauxite, coal, copper, gold, iron ore, lead, manganese, nickel, opals, silver, tin, tungsten, uranium, zinc), agriculture, pastoral products, petroleum products.

CANADA

Imports: mostly manufactured goods — auto parts and machinery, fabricated metals and materials, metal ores and concentrates.

Exports: motor vehicles and parts; pulp, newsprint, and lumber; food, especially wheat; fuel, especially petroleum; metallic minerals, mainly nickel, copper, iron ore, zinc; nonmetallic minerals, predominantly asbestos

CHINA

Imports: grain, foodstuff, machinery, automobiles, airplanes.

Exports: rice, soybean, corn, meat, raw materials, fuels, manufactured goods.

HONG KONG

Imports: basic necessities — textiles, basic manufactured goods, rice, iron and steel, petroleum products, textiles and textile fibres, chemicals, cement, building material, paper.

Exports: mainly oil; also timber, rubber, coffee, tin, palm oil, tea, tobacco, bauxite, copper, nickel.

JAPAN

Imports: raw materials and fuel mostly; also iron, copper, zinc, manganese, bauxite ores, wood, cotton and woolen fibres, oil seeds.

Exports: motor vehicles, iron and steel, ships, electrical and electronic equipment, nonelectrical machinery, cameras.

MALAYSIA

Imports: food, especially grain; machinery and other manufactured goods, petroleum products.

Exports: rubber, tin, palm oil, timber, bauxite, petrol, rice, coconuts.

NEW ZEALAND

Imports: machine and transportation equipment, basic manufactured goods, mineral fuels, coffee, tea, fruits, textile fibres.

Exports: mostly pastoral products — dairy products, wool, meat; also logs, paper, wood pulp.

PHILIPPINES

Imports: machine and transportation equipment, textiles, iron and steel products, foodstuffs.

Exports: foodstuffs and raw materials — sugar, copra, coconut, wood products, metallic minerals, lumber.

SINGAPORE

Imports: raw materials, rice.

Exports: mostly petroleum products.

SOUTH KOREA

Imports: raw materials, semifinished goods, food, crude oil, heavy machinery, chemicals.
Exports: industrial products — sweaters, plywood, electrical appliances, wigs, footwear.

TAIWAN

Imports: electrical materials, machinery and tools, ores, metals, chemicals, vehicles, parts.
Exports: textiles, electrical equipment, wood products, nonelectrical machinery, metals.

THAILAND

Imports: petroleum, iron and steel, chemicals, machine and transportation equipment.
Exports: mostly foodstuff, such as tapioca, corn, rice; natural gas, natural rubber, tin, jute, teak, kenalf fibre.

UNITED STATES

Imports: mineral fuels — crude petroleum and petroleum products, transportation and telecommunication equipment.
Exports: food and live animals, machinery — electrical equipment, office machinery, and computers.

Sources: various issues of *Asiaweek* and *Far Eastern Economic Review.*

APPENDIX TABLE 12
B.C. EXPORTS TO PACIFIC RIM
1980
($Cdn)

Commodity	Total (000s)	% of Total Exports
Aluminum	357,130	80.5
Asbestos	34,942	41.6
Coal	460,258	89.3
Copper	317,088	85.0
Fish	90,124	32.8
Lead	5,682	7.0
Lumber	553,149	22.5
Paper	189,545	24.6
Wood pulp	575,273	30.3
Zinc	24,247	17.5

N.B. — includes exports to Mexico, Pacific South, and Central Americas.

Source: Pacific Rim Export Markets: A B.C. Perspective
(Victoria, B.C.: Ministry of Industry and Small Business, 1984), p. 3.

APPENDIX TABLE 13
B.C. EXPORTS TO PACIFIC RIM COUNTRIES, 1982
($CDN MILLIONS)

Country	Commodity											
	Apples	Aluminum	Asbestos	Coal	Copper	Fish	Lumber Products	Parts, Mach., & Equipment	Paper Products	Sulphur	Wood pulp	Zinc
Australia	–	–	7.9	–	–	11.6	52.3	–	30.7	3.5	25.0	–
China	–	51.0	–	1.6	–	–	9.9	–	2.4	0.5	67.1	20.3
Hong Kong	1.5	59.2	–	6.1	–	–	–	–	8.3	–	9.5	1.8
Indonesia	–	3.3	–	–	–	–	–	4.7	10.0	–	7.8	6.3
Japan	–	148.3	–	564.6	230.8	159.7	384.5	–	–	–	331.3	–
Malaysia	0.2	3.8	4.8	–	–	–	–	–	14.3	–	0.2	2.5
New Zealand	–	–	1.2	–	–	4.4	2.7	3.0	–	2.1	–	4.7
Philippines	–	0.7	–	–	–	–	–	12.1	1.3	–	3.4	4.6
Singapore	0.4	–	1.0	–	–	–	–	2.3	11.0	–	–	4.3
South Korea	–	7.5	–	110.6	17.4	2.7	–	3.9	1.2	–	20.0	–
Thailand	–	8.9	1.7	–	–	–	–	0.1	2.7	–	3.7	3.8

Source: Pacific Rim Export Markets: Country Profiles, A B.C. Perspective.
(Victoria, B.C.: Ministry of Industry and Small Business, 1984), various pages.

APPENDIX TABLE 14
CANADA: TOURIST ARRIVALS (000s) AND RECEIPTS ($US millions)
1975-1980

	Arrivals						Receipts					
	1975	1976	1977	1978	1979	1980	1975	1976	1977	1978	1979	1980
Australia	516	532	563	631	793	904	300	295	347	456	531	725
Canada	13,625	13,017	12,694	12,745	12,615	12,426	1,534	1,641	1,616	1,722	2,008	2,284*
Hong Kong	1,301	1,560	1,730	2,030	2,188	2,279	525	740	786	1,110	1,279	1,317
Indonesia	372	401	433	469	501	561	34	40	42	131	209	246*
Japan	708	795	668	659	685	844	252	313	425	470	554	644
South Korea	547	834	950	1,079	1,126	976	141	275	370	408	326	369
Malaysia	1,180	1,225	667*	723*	732*	791*	31	35	39	50	41*	46*
New Zealand	243	384	390	407	432	465	132	154	155	166	186	226
Philippines	502	615	715	842	896	964	155	235	128	210	238	320
Singapore	1,029	1,162	1,636	2,016	2,247	2,562	264	283	388	446	636	845
Thailand	1,180	1,098	1,214	1,448	1,586	1,847	224	197	205	435	549	867
United States	15,698	17,523	18,610	19,842	20,310	22,500	4,876	5,806	6,150	7,186	8,335	10,100
TOTAL	36,901	39,147	40,270	42,891	44,111	47,119	8,768	10,014	10,651	12,790	14,892	17,989

*Estimated figures.

Source: 1981 Statistical Yearbook, United Nations, pp. 1041-42 for 1977-80 figures.
1979/80 Statistical Yearbook, United Nations, pp. 532-33 for 1975-76 figures.

APPENDIX TABLE 15
BY COUNTRY OR AREA OF NATIONALITY
1980
(000s)

Country of Nationality	Country of Arrival											
	AUS	CDA	HK	IND	JAP	MAL	NZ	PH	S'PORE	S.KOR	THAI	US
Australia	–	57.9	166.2	82.0	27.5	110.4*	217.7	68.5	239.2	4.8	64.2	225.0
Canada	28.5	–	56.4	8.6	41.0	18.3	18.6	1.9	20.9	8.4	17.8	11,385.0
Hong Kong	–	–	–	–	–	–	–	–	–	–	–	–
Indonesia	12.7	–	79.4	–	22.4	56.9	1.7	10.5	371.8	5.4	27.9	1,125.0
Japan	48.8	124.1	472.2	61.7	–	113.5	19.2	260.5	287.4	468.4	225.4	–
Malaysia	16.4	–	99.9	47.7	20.3	–	2.1	28.8	481.5	10.1	402.5	–
New Zealand	307.1	17.4	28.2	7.9	5.4	–*	–	4.5	63.0	0.9	9.7	105.0
Philippines	4.9	12.9	98.6	5.9	42.9	18.3	0.7	–	48.1	6.2	34.1	–
Singapore	16.4	–	89.7	61.2	18.4	312.9	3.6	32.1	–	5.0	67.6	–
South Korea	–	–	–	–	–	–	–	–	–	–	–	–
Thailand	4.4	–	148.7	11.1	21.3	456.3	–	9.9	93.7	7.5	–	–
United States	111.4	10,573.6	346.9	52.6	319.0	69.7	77.8	177.5	135.8	121.4	115.3	–

*New Zealand and Australia data

Sources: 1981 Statistical Yearbook, United Nations, pp. 1046-60.
    Statistical Yearbook for Asia and the Pacific, 1980, various pages.

APPENDIX TABLE 16

MAIL TRAFFIC
1974-1978
(millions)

		1974	1975	1976	1977	1978
Canada	A	165,647	130,447	149,446	150,644	178,662
	B	113,563	103,981	137,804	138,404	121,250
Hong Kong	A	58,206	57,608	59,642	62,026	69,590
	B	76,739	76,132	78,002	78,892	88,468
Indonesia	A	26,222	26,964	17,686	35,448	32,908
	B	12,135	11,505	10,430	11,986	11,842
Malaysia	A	65,551	62,012	60,469	62,011	66,610
	B	47,340	48,741	55,.011	55,660	60,238
South Korea	A	45,034	43,140	47,186	56,523	—
	B	18,586	20,394	19,471	30,602	—
Thailand	A	25,960	24,752	24,333	23,976	25,034
	B	15,944	13,540	14,519	13,485	14,627
Australia	A	193,176	190,800	202,483	149,393	149,278
	B	109,863	102,300	103,783	84,993	81,433
New Zealand	A	72,728	64,575	64,735	62,834	70,436
	B	40,738	41,025	37,210	38,042	37,328
United States	A	1,594,000	1,766,000	—	—	—
	B	960,389	922,971	—	—	—

A: foreign received; B: foreign sent.

Source: 1979/80 Statistical Yearbook, United Nations, pp. 608-17.

APPENDIX TABLE 17

TELEGRAMS
Foreign Sent
(millions)

	1974	1975	1976	1977	1978	1979	1980
Canada	1652	1675	1434	1298	1201	1142	1162
Indonesia	469	440	382	336	288	251	232
Japan	3240	3051	2929	2793	2540	2356	2034
Malaysia	537	484	449	406	382	387	345
Singapore	1098	938	859	797	736	699	652
South Korea	465	722	725	665	553	270	—
Thailand	547	473	442	405	369	219	—
Australia	261	2430	2208	2072	1902	1754	1626
New Zealand	1110	1021	914	836	837	837	810
Philippines	—	—	—	1513	830	689	582
Hong Kong	1255	1225	1156	1094	1261	1360	1390
China	—	580	732	745	655	734	780
United States	8583	7878	7457	7290	7294	7240	6871

Source: 1981 Statistical Yearbook, United Nations, pp. 990-93.

APPENDIX TABLE 18
TELEPHONES
(000s)

		1975	1976*	1977*	1978	1979	1980
Canada	A	13,165	13,885	14,488	15,172	15,839	16,531
	B	57.2	59.6	61.8	64.3	66.5	68.6
Hong Kong	A	1,034	1,132	1,251	1,382	1,517	1,676
	B	23.5	25.5	27.8	29.3	30.2	32.6
Indonesia	A	305	319	347	393	441	487
	B	.2	.2	.3	.3	.3	.3
Japan	A	39,405	43,232	46,308	48,646	51,072	53,634
	B	35.6	38.4	40.8	42.4	44.2	46.0
Malaysia	A	292	330	375	439	507	598
	B	2.5	2.7	2.9	3.3	3.8	4.5
Singapore	A	318	329	395	540	625	702
	B	14.1	14.4	17.1	23.1	26.5	29.1
South Korea	A	1,400	1,643	1,976	2,387	2,898	—
	B	4.0	4.6	5.4	6.5	7.7	—
Thailand	A	312	334	367	409	451	497
	B	.7	.8	.8	.9	1.0	1.1
Australia	A	5,267	5,502	5,835	6,266	6,677	7,153
	B	39.0	39.5	41.5	44.0	46.3	48.9
New Zealand	A	1,531	1,610	1,674	1,715	1,762	1,730
	B	49.6	51.5	53.3	54.5	56.0	55.0
China	A	3,412	—	—	3,972	4,151	4,355
	B	—	—	—	.4	.4	.4
Philippines	A	448	—	—	600	628	702
	B	1.1	—	—	1.3	1.3	1.5
United States	A	149,011	155,173	162,072	169,027	175,536	180,424
	B	68.6	71.8	74.4	75.5	77.5	78.8

A: number in use; B: per 100 inhabitants.

Source: 1981 Statistical Yearbook, United Nations, pp. 995-97.
    *Years 1976, 1977 from 1979/80 Statistical Yearbook, pp. 623-26.

APPENDIX TABLE 19
MOTOR VEHICLES IN USE
(000s)

		1974	1975	1976	1977	1978	1979	1980
Canada	A	8,328.4	8,692.8	9,016.3	9,554.0	9,745.0	9,985.1	10,255.5
	B	2,016.1	2,177.4	2,318.6	2,494.3	2,770.0	2,907.3	2,955.3
Hong Kong	A	125.3	120.3	120.0	130.0	149.7	171.5	200.0
	B	41.0	44.5	46.6	52.2	57.1	61.5	69.2
Indonesia	A	337.8	383.1	420.9	479.3	535.6	581.5	639.5
	B	197.9	231.5	263.1	327.1	392.6	462.9	560.1
Japan	A	15,853.0	17,236.0	18,457.0	19,826.0	21,280.0	22,667.0	23,659.0
	B	10,497.1	10,315.0	11,011.0	11,553.0	12,228.0	12,600.0	13,193.0
Malaysia	A	366.1	407.3	447.1	502.8	566.0	–	–
	B	122.4	137.6	151.6	167.0	183.5	–	–
Philippines	A	362.5	383.3	386.2	416.4	464.0	–	–
	B	247.3	273.2	281.0	315.6	369.8	–	–
Singapore	A	149.0	149.0	142.1	142.1	146.4	–	–
	B	41.2	46.3	51.0	54.9	61.5	–	–
South Korea	A	76.5	106.3	129.4	125.6	184.9	241.4	249.1
	B	96.9	87.6	89.5	99.8	192.5	244.5	269.4
Thailand	A	295.7	266.1	270.9	–	–	–	–
	B	250.7	246.2	296.9	–	–	–	–
Australia	A	4,995.8	5,468.4	5,937.1	6,367.5	6,819.0	–	–
	B	1,191.2	1,311.8	1,449.5	1,580.6	1,707.7	–	–
New Zealand	A	1,087.0	1,138.1	1,180.6	1,234.1	1,251.6	1,280.8	1,322.5
	B	209.7	217.0	221.7	244.1	249.7	261.3	266.7
China	A	90.3	112.8	134.2	149.1	171.1	196.8	237.8
	B	649.8	753.6	869.2	978.1	1,108.5	1,264.7	1,436.2
United States	A	104,228.9	106,075.9	110,188.6	112,287.5	116,575.0	116,573.4	118,458.7
	B	23,722.4	26,242.8	28,257.8	30,092.9	32,203.0	31.841.2	33,410.6

A: passenger vehicles; B: commercial vehicles.

Source: 1981 Statistical Yearbook, United Nations, pp. 1006-11.

Appendix 1

"Overseas Chinese Investment in Real Estate Around the Pacific Rim"
Areas/Topics to be Covered in Interviews and Case Studies

A. *Investment Flows*
   1. Origins and Destinations
   2. Magnitudes
      a) Around the Pacific
      b) Between the most important origins and destinations

B. *Investment Criteria — Local v. Overseas* (compare)
   1. Risk
   2. Return
   3. Part of Investment Portfolio or Seen in Isolation
   4. Time Horizon of Investment
   5. Non-economic Criteria
      a) Family members located in area or presence of previous business associates
      b) Political stability
      c) Foreign ownership legislation and institutional impediments/ incentives
      d) Inheritance taxes
      e) Tax treaties and treatment of overseas investment
      f) Ease of financing
      g) Immigration policy

C. *Information Sources and Methods of Analysis and Evaluation*
   1. Sources of Information and Types of Information Required
   2. Methods of Assessing Reliability of Information
   3. Analysis of Information
      a) Formal methods of investment analysis
      b) Rules of thumb
      c) Intuition and "gut" feel

D. *Method of Investing*
   1. Leverage and Sources of Financing and Extent of Borrowing
   2. Transfer of Funds
      a) How?
      b) By whom?
   3. Transfer of Title
      a) To whom (registered company, local agent, direct ownership from abroad)?
      b) Use of local legal people and how chosen
   4. Use of Income Earnings (kept locally, remitted home, invested elsewhere)
   5. Migration to Investment Destination

E. *Selling Assets*
   1. Criteria
   2. Information Needs
   3. Evaluation of Offers
   4. Completing the Sale
      a) Use of local agents and legal assistance
      b) Disposing of proceeds of sale

Appendix 2

1983 Survey for SPS International Properties Ltd. (Hong Kong)
A Study of Investment Abroad

sample = 120,000 Hong Kong people, a proper cross-section

WHY INVEST

	under 39 years old	over 39 years old
citizenship	12%	5%
future uncertain	37	26

Thus, people under 39 years of age want to move because they fear for their future in Hong Kong. Those over 40 are less willing to move because they feel that they will not have too long to live under Communist rule (before they die); a more important reason for moving would be to assure a better future for their families.

72% OF THE SAMPLE OWN HONG KONG PROPERTY AND NOW WANT TO INVEST OVERSEAS. THE TOP FIVE CHOICES ARE:

USA	43%
Canada	34
Australia	17
Singapore	7
United Kingdom	4

WITHIN THE U.S. AND CANADA, PREFERRED CITIES ARE:

USA

Los Angeles/San Francisco	49%
New York	28
Other	19

CANADA

Toronto	43%
Vancouver	32
Other	3
Don't know	43

WHERE PEOPLE'S RELATIVES LIVE:

USA		39%
San Francisco	10%	
New York	10	
Los Angeles	4	
California	4	
Other	3	
Unknown	8	

CANADA		28%
Toronto	13%	
Vancouver	6	
Other	3	
Unknown	6	

AUSTRALIA		9%
Sydney	6%	
Other	2	
Unknown	1	

UNITED KINGDOM	8%
SINGAPORE	6
PHILIPPINES	4
TAIWAN	4
MALAYSIA	3

Thus, on the basis of preferred residence and location of relatives, the top five choices in which people would like to invest seem to be Toronto, San Francisco, New York, Vancouver, and Sydney.

Canadian cities would appear to be favoured more because Canada is the favoured educational location, provides a pleasant climate, has good growth potential, offers political stability, and will provide for the safety of the family future.

WHY BUY ABROAD

	Already Invested	Intend to Buy
Uncertain future	40%	50%
Citizenship	15	25
Retire	6	13
Climate/environment	3	8
Better living	3	5
Children's future	2	1
Political stability	2	3
Poor living conditions at home	1	0

WHY PEOPLE HAVE ALREADY INVESTED ABROAD

Because of uncertain future	55%
To make money	45

CORPORATE INVESTORS (19% of sample)

	Already Invested	Intend to Buy
USA	50%	39%
Canada	33	39
Singapore	17	6
Australia	17	0
United Kingdom	11	0
Other	39	34

N.B. Totals may equal more than 100 because people have invested in more than one place.

Source: Interview with Anton Koschany, Producer, *The Fifth Estate*, by Cheryl Wong.

Bibliography

BOOKS AND BOOK CHAPTERS

Adachi, Ken. *The Enemy That Never Was.* Toronto: McClelland and Stewart, 1976.

The author attempts to indicate, with as much documentation as possible, what it was like to have immigrated to Canada or to have been born in Canada as a member of what was initially an unpopular minority group — the Japanese.

Included is an examination of the Canadian government's actions during W.W. II involving the evacuation and detention of people of Japanese origin from the coastal area of British Columbia.

Amyot, Jacques. *The Manila Chinese.* Quezon City, Philippines: Institute of Philippine Culture, 1973.

The Chinese community of Manila: a study of the adaption of Chinese familism to the Philippine environment.

Baker, Hugh D. R. *Chinese Family and Kinship.* New York: Columbia University Press, 1979.

The author examines the traditional Chinese family and its inner workings: family composition, lineage, ancestor worship, and the relation of the family and lineage to Chinese state and society. The central theme is that the family revolves around a generation-age-sex hierarchy, with the elder males ranking the highest.

Balazs, Etienne. *Chinese Civilization and Bureaucracy*, New Haven, Conn.: Yale University Press, 1964.

A collection of the author's essays dealing with major themes in Chinese history: the role of the scholar-official class; the structure of Chinese institutions as they were shaped by the elite and modified by changing circumstances; the distinctive character of Chinese commercial and industrial life; the varieties of protest and dissent.

Barak, Ronald. *Foreign Investment in U.S. Real Estate.* New York: Law and Business, 1981.

An explanation of what the foreign investor will encounter when investing in U.S. real estate. There is a brief overview of the current investment activity, followed by an explanation of traditional investment motives and the taxation and regulation of foreign investors. The different investment alternatives are discussed in more detail, along with a survey of U.S. real estate. Various sample documents in the appendices conclude the book.

Beattie, Hilary J. *Land and Lineage in China.* Cambridge, Mass.: Harvard University Press, 1979.

An historical study of social structure and social mobility on the local level — a case study of T'ung-ch'eng County, Anhwei in the Ming and Ch'ing Dynasties. Book focusses on the subject of landholding and the role it played in the formation of the Chinese elite ruling class. Also deals with the composition of this elite and the role played by large kinship groups and the intermarriage among them.

Bonavia, David. *The Chinese.* New York: Penguin, 1982.

The author's description of the life of the Chinese in the People's Republic of China. As well as examining the people themselves, the author also looks at the environment in which they live and its effects on them.

Chen, Edward K. Y. Hyper-growth in Asian Economics. London: Macmillan, 1979.

An empirical analysis of the growth experience of five fast-growing Asian economies; namely Hong Kong, Japan, Korea, Singapore and Taiwan. The book deals with the testing of growth and development theories in the light of the experience of the selected economies.

Cheng, Tong Yung. *The Economy of Hong Kong.* Hong Kong: Far East Publications, 1982.

The book covers Hong Kong from economic (micro and macro), social, and political viewpoints. The author states that Hong Kong's tremendous economic growth is unique because it has occurred in an environment of industrialization where the government operates with a laissez-faire policy.
Thus, industrialization can still occur within a classical economy. Also studies the impact of China's Four Modernizations programme on Hong Kong.

Chin, John M. *The Sarawak Chinese.* Kuala Lumpur: Oxford University Press, 1981.
Reviews the history of the Chinese in Sarawak with some analysis of present status and political participation. Good historical analysis, generalizable to other overseas Chinese communities.

Cohen, R. B. "The new international division of labor, multinational corporations and urban hierarchy." In M. Dear and A. Scott, editors, *Urbanization and Urban Planning in Capitalist Society*, New York: Methuen, 1981:287-315.

The new international division of labour involves an international system for producing goods and services primarily accomplished by the largest multinational firms. A key element in this new order is the growing importance of the newly industrialized nations as centres for productive activities. This essay examines the subject and discusses how it has affected corporations, financial institutions, national economies, and the world's urban centres.

Coppel, Charles A. *The Chinese in Indonesia, The Philippines and Malaysia.* London: Minority Rights Group, 1982.

This short study documents the status of the Chinese communities in Indonesia, The Philippines, and Malaysia. In all these countries the Chinese are economically privileged on average and treated with hostility.

Cyert, Richard M., and James G. March. *A Behavioral Theory of the Firm.* Englewood Cliffs, N.J.: Prentice-Hall, 1963.

The book deals with the business firm and the way it makes economic decisions. The authors make detailed observations of the procedures by which firms make these decisions and use these observations as a basis for a theory of decision-making within business organizations. Process-oriented models of firms are developed and then subjected to empirical testing against the actual behaviour of identifiable firms. From this a summary set of concepts and relations is developed into a theory with generality beyond the specific firms studied.

Daly, M. T. *Sydney Boom, Sydney Bust.* Sydney: Allen and Unwin, 1982.
This book deals with the real estate market in Sydney, Australia, and the changes which have occurred in the market since the middle of the 1960's.

Dear, Michael, and Allen J. Scott, editors. *Urbanization and Urban Planning in Capitalist Society.* New York: Methuen, 1981.

Collection of essays which look at urbanization and planning in western societies. Authors suggest that this process is a function of capitalist system and the international development of that system.

De Glopper, Donald R. "Doing business in Lukang." In W. E. Willmott, editor. *Economic Organization in Chinese Society.* Stanford: Stanford University Press, 1972: 297-326.

Case Study of the business community in a small port city on the west coast of Taiwan.

Donges, Juergen, Bernd Stecher, and Frank Wolter. *Industrial Development Policies for Indonesia.* Tubingen: Institut fur Weltwirtschaft an der Universitat Kiel, 1974.

A study of the current industrialization patterns in Indonesia. The authors make projections for the future, both in the medium and the long run.
Included in the chapter on current industrialization is a section on foreign direct investment, which concludes that the Indonesian government should continue attracting ethnic Chinese investment through incentives.

Eberhard, Wolfram. *A History of China — from the earliest times to the present day.* Los Angeles: University of California Press, 1960.

This is a social history of China, presenting the main lines of development of the Chinese social structure from the earliest times to the present day.
The text is based upon the study of original Chinese sources, the work of modern Chinese and Japanese scholars, and also the research of western scholars.

FitzGerald, Stephen. *China and the Overseas Chinese.* Cambridge: Cambridge University Press, 1972.

An examination of the policy of the People's Republic of China towards the overseas Chinese — those people of Chinese origin living outside China, mostly in Southeast Asia. The author traces the development of this policy from 1949-1970.

FitzGerald, Stephen. *China and the World.* Canberra: Australian National University Press, 1977.

Author offers an interpretation of China's approach to the world outside its own boundaries and the difficulties most western governments experience in coming to terms with China. Against the background of past and contemporary Chinese history, the author analyses present-day China's approach to specific countries: the U.S. and the Soviet Union, Southeast Asia, Japan, and Australia.

Freedman, Maurice. *The Study of Chinese Society.* Stanford: Stanford University Press, 1979.

A series of 24 essays dealing with:
(a) The Chinese in Southeast Asia
(b) Chinese Society in Singapore
(c) Social Change in the New Territories of Hong Kong
(d) Kinship and Religion in China
(e) The Study of Chinese Society.

Fröbel, F., J. Heinrichs, and B. Kreye. *The New International Division of Labour.* Cambridge: Cambridge University Press, 1980.

This book first advanced the NIDL thesis. The internationalization of West German industry is the focus of the analysis. The authors trace the movement of such industries as textiles to underdeveloped low wage regions from advanced economies and their high wages.

Fung-shuen, Victor Sit, and Koichi Mera, editors. *Urbanization and National Development in Asia.* Hong Kong: University of Hong Kong, 1982.

A collection of papers dealing with the relationship between urbanization and national development and the associated policy dimensions and implications. The papers are grouped into three major categories:
(a) Japan, Korea, and Taiwan
(b) Developing Southeast Asia
(c) City-states and the Capital City Region.

Geiger, Theodore, and Frances M. Geiger. *Tales of Two City-States: The Development Progress of Hong Kong and Singapore.* Washington, D.C.: National Planning Association, 1973.

An account of the development progress of Hong Kong and Singapore. The analysis is based on three types of sources: interviews; personal visits to businesses, schools, and factories; and official statistics.

Gilbert, Alan, and Josef Gugler. *Cities, Poverty and Development — Urbanization in the Third World.* London: Oxford University Press, 1981.

This study presents a comprehensive account of Third World urbanization including: the evolution of Third World Cities as part of the world system, the nature of urban and regional disparities within countries, the causes and patterns of rural-urban migration, the structure of urban labour markets, the urban housing market, urban ways of life and the adoption of migrants, various patterns of political conflict, and current issues in urban and regional planning.

Greenblatt, Sidney L., R.W. Wilson, and A.A. Wilson. *Social Interaction in Chinese Society.* New York: Praeger, 1982.

Series of nine articles on sociological issues in China and Taiwan.

Hofheinz, Roy, Jr., and Kent E. Calder. *The Eastasia Edge.* New York: Basic, 1982.
The authors examine the success of Eastasian countries (Japan, China, North and South Korea, Singapore, and Hong Kong) in the business world. Policies and common cultural values of both the East and the West are compared.

Horwood, Peter, editor. *Foreign Investment in Land — Alternative Controls.* Research Monograph #4, Vancouver, B.C.: Urban Land Economics Division, University of British Columbia, 1976.

Proceedings of conference held in Vancouver to discuss foreign investment controls. Papers included on analysis of legislation in Saskatchewan and P.E.I., an overview of the whole question of foreign ownership and the need to control it, and the magnitude of the problem.

Hsia, Ronald, Henry Ho, and Edwin Lim. *The Structure and Growth of the Hong Kong Economy.* Hamburg: Institute of Asian Affairs, 1975.

Authors provide an inter-industry data based analysis of the structure of the Hong Kong economy and its growth as an industrialized economy in the trading world. Data on the interrelationship among the various sectors of the economy are derived from both published and unpublished sources and supplemented by interviews and surveys.

Hsia, Ronald, and Lawrence Chau. *Industrialisation, Employment and Income Distribution.* London: Croom Helm, 1978.

A case study of Hong Kong and how its economic growth and development have affected income distribution. The authors find that during the 1960's income distribution became more equal than it had been in the 1950's.

Hughes, Richard. *Borrowed Place, Borrowed Time.* Harmondsworth, England: Penguin, 1968.

A classic book about Hong Kong's precarious situation. The author traces the history of Hong Kong, delineates its problems, and evaluates its future prospects in light of its return to China in 1997.

Hughes, Helen, ed. *Foreign Investment and Industrialization in Singapore.* Madison: University of Wisconsin Press, 1969.

A series of papers dealing with the investment climate and industrial status in Singapore. Private investment by overseas Chinese from Hong Kong, Indonesia, the Philippines, and Malaysia is covered. Concludes that Singapore does not need to offer direct financial incentives because of its central location, amenities, and public services already provided.

King, Ambrose Y. C., Rance P. L. Lee, editors. *Social Life and Development in Hong Kong.* Shatin, Hong Kong: Chinese University of Hong Kong, 1981.

A series of essays written through a 10-year span regarding the socialization and development of Hong Kong. The book is divided into two sections: metropolitan structural development and institutional characteristics and their changes. Each attempt to explain the phenomenon of social and political stability within a system that has been constantly changing at a breakneck pace since the 1950s.

Kirby, Stuart. *Towards the Pacific Century: Economic Development in the Pacific Basin.* London: The Economist Intelligence Unit Limited, 1983.

A review of the explosive growth of the Pacific Rim economy and a prospective look into the future role the region will play. The author concludes that the region is likely to be a dominant force by the next century.

Lethbridge, David, ed. *The Business Environment in Hong Kong.* Hong Kong: Oxford University Press, 1980.

This book explains the government policy of "positive non-interventionism ...in the context of the economic, social and political...business environment," stressing the importance of the workforce. Further chapters discuss the financial and legal workings from the viewpoint of foreign investment, using them to help explain Hong Kong's phenomenal economic growth in recent years.

Lim, Linda Y.C., and L.A. Peter Gosling, editors. *The Chinese in Southeast Asia, Volumes 1 (Ethnicity and Economic Activity) and 2 (Identity, Culture and Politics),* Singapore: Maruzen, 1983.

This is an excellent selection of essays (thirteen in each volume). Together they provide valuable insights into the relationship between Chinese ethnic values and economic activity and success, as well as rooting these activities firmly in their cultural and political context. Numerous case studies provide the basis for the papers in the books. This yields excellent documentation of many of the characteristics ascribed to overseas Chinese.

Lindblom, Charles E. "The science of muddling through." *Public Administration Review,* 19(2):79-88, reprinted in John H. Turner, Alan C. Filley and Robert J. House, editors, *Studies in Managerial Process and Organization Behavior.* Glenview, Ill.: Scott, Foresman, 1959.

A classic article which suggests that decision-makers do not try to optimize but rather rely heavily on intuition.

Logan, M.I., and Maurice T. Daly. *The International Finance System and Economic Development.* Sydney: Department of Geography, 1984.

The decline in fixed exchange rates is analysed in the context of growing international debt and the development of such leading capital markets as Hong Kong and Singapore.

McFadyen, Stuart, and Robert Hobart. "The economic implications of foreign ownership of Canadian land." In Michael Walker and Lawrence B. Smith, editors. *Public Property?* Vancouver, B.C.: Fraser Institute, 1977:179-203.

Article deals with the question of foreign ownership of Canadian lands. Issues addressed include: extent of foreign ownership, type of lands held, and the effects on land prices and taxes.

Marr, William L., and Donald G. Paterson. *Canada: An Economic History.* Toronto: Macmillan of Canada.

This definitive economic history of Canada documents the extent to which Canada has relied on "staples" (resources) to achieve its economic growth.

Thus, the present Canadian reliance on resource exports is firmly rooted in Canadian economic history.

Motha, Philip. "Outlook for property in the 1980's." *Reprints 1980/81.* Singapore: Department of Building and Estate Management, National University of Singapore, 1981:67-82.

Concludes that the land ownership problem will worsen in the future; the solution is government land banking with development rights leased out. Most of the property market will experience increasing values because of rising demand and the construction of the Mass Transit Railway.

_____, ed. *Valuation and Land Economy in Singapore.* Singapore: University Education Press, 1976.

A four-part book covering real estate in general, property valuation, the real estate market, and estate management and development. The real estate market segment covers such topics as property development trends, peculiarities of investment, speculation about whether or not the market has reached rock-bottom, property prospects, and the property situation.

Olsen, Stephen M. "The inculcation of economic values in Taipei business families." In W. E. Willmott, editor. *Economic Organization in Chinese Society.* Stanford: Stanford University Press, 1972:261-96.

This paper examines two major concepts — economic values and economic socialization — on the basis of questionnaire responses from a study conducted in Taiwan during 1967-68.

Omohundro, John T. *Chinese Merchant Families in Iloilo.* Athens: The Ohio University Press, 1981.

A case study of the Chinese population that live in an urban community (Iloilo City) in The Philippines. The book is organized around three central areas; the organization and operation of Chinese business life, the family business, and the prospect of Chinese integration into Filipino society.

Ouchi, William. *Theory Z.* Reading, Mass.: Addison-Wesley, 1981.

Author deals with a type of Japanese management style known as Theory Z.

Parsons, Melinda J. *Hong Kong 1983.* Hong Kong: Government Information Services, 1983.

The book gives current information on the economic, social, and political status of Hong Kong. Also covered is its history and environment. Relevant are the chapters dealing with the financial system and economy and housing and land. More detailed data may be extracted from the appendices found at the end of the book.

Pascale, Richard T., and Anthony G. Athos. *The Art of Japanese Management.* New York: Simon and Schuster, 1981.

The book examines the Japanese style of business management and the reasons behind its general success.

Potter, Jack M. *Capitalism and The Chinese Peasant: Social and Economic Change in a Hong Kong Village.* Berkeley and Los Angeles: University of California Press, 1968.

The book documents the evolution of a village as it moved from peasant status toward a commercial centre. The roles of family, kinship, handling of money are all discussed and analysed.

Purcell, Victor. *The Chinese in Southeast Asia.* Second Edition. Kuala Lumpur: Oxford University Press, 1965.

The author relates the history of the Chinese in Southeast Asia, from the 1300s-1960s. Chinese in the various countries (Burma, Thailand, Cambodia, Malaysia, British Borneo, Indonesia, and The Philippines) are reviewed according to immigration patterns, economic activities, interrelationships with locals and with government (Europeans, Chinese, and national).

Rating and Valuation Department. *Property Review 1983.* Hong Kong: Government Printer, 1983.

A summary of the property market in the last year states that some projects have been deferred owing to economic downturn and predicts that there will be oversupply in all sectors in the coming year.

Salaff, Janet W. "Marriage relationships as a resource: Singapore Chinese families." In Sidney L. Greenblatt, Richard W. Wilson, and Amy Averbacher Wilson, editors. *Social Interaction in Chinese Society.* New York: Praeger, 1982.

Scharfstein, Ben-Ami. *The Mind of China.* New York: Dell, 1974.

The author examines the ideas and customs of Chinese society — including Chinese art, history, cosmography, and philosophy.

Silin, Robert H. "Marketing and credit in a Hong Kong wholesale market." In W.E. Willmott, editor. *Economic Organization in Chinese Society.* Stanford: Stanford University Press, 1972:327-52.

Case study of the organization of a Hong Kong wholesale vegetable market. The author analyses the relative influence of ascriptive ties and various criteria of performance on the organization of economic activity among small-and medium-scale Chinese traders. Also looked at the factors that maintain systems of reciprocity in economic relations.

Singapore: Facts and Figures 1981. Singapore: Information Division, Ministry of Culture, 1981.

Supplies brief, very general information about Singapore. The section on the economy is especially relevant. Other topics such as land and people, government, trade, industry, finance, health and welfare, public housing, tourism, and international relations are also covered.

Skinner, G. William, and A. Thomas Kirsch, editors. *Change and Persistence in Thai Society.* Ithaca, N.Y.: Cornell University Press, 1984.

This collection of essays is primarily concerned with Thai society as a whole. However, the Thai Chinese are featured prominently in several papers because of their key economic role.

Stanback, Thomas M., Jr., and Thierry J. Noyelle. *Cities in Transition.* Totowa, N.J.: Allanheld, Osmun, 1982.

This study seeks to identify some of the critical dimensions of change undergone by metropolitan labour markets during the 1970s through a comparative analysis of seven urban areas: Atlanta, Denver, Buffalo, Phoenix, Columbus, Nashville, and Charlotte.

Stover, Leon. *The Cultural Ecology of Chinese Civilization.* New York: Mentor Books, 1974.

The book examines traditional Chinese society, its structure, its dynamics, its mores and its morality. Other issues dealt with are: the changes the Communist regime has wrought on the country, the historical currents that influence Chinese policy, and the differences between traditional China and the West.

Souther, Michael, ed. *Australia in the Seventies.* Ringwood, Australia: Penguin, 1972.

After riding the crest of an economic boom for almost twenty years, the Australians experienced an economic downtown in 1970, causing a re-evaluation of domestic and international policies. This book attempts to reflect what has happened and makes some predictions about the future. Chapters on money and society include articles relevant to both capital flows and real estate.

Utrecht, Ernst, and Kate Short. *Transnational Corporations in South East Asia.* 2 vols. Sydney: University of Sydney, Transnational Corporations Research Project, 1978.

Two volumes containing papers written on transnationals in South East Asia. Of particular interest are the papers titled: "Australian Based Manufacturing Companies in Indonesia" and "Australian Based Manufacturing Companies in Singapore." Ideas brought up in these papers regarding investment motives and tax implications may be generally applied.

Vogel, Ezra. *Japan as Number One.* Cambridge, Mass.: Harvard University Press, 1979.

Author discusses Japan's rise to dominant economic position. Analyses why Japan has been so successful.

Ward, Barbara E. "A small factory in Hong Kong: Some aspects of its internal organization." In W. E. Willmott, editor. *Economic Organization in Chinese Society.* Stanford: Stanford University Press, 1972:353-86.

Case study which addresses the issue of industrialization in Hong Kong.

Ward, Peter. *White Canada Forever.* Montreal: McGill-Queen's University Press, 1978.

Deals with racism and Canadian immigration policy. Traces the history of these policies with a focus on Japanese and Chinese.

Watson, James L. *Emigration and the Chinese Lineage: The Mans in Hong Kong and London.* Berkeley and Los Angeles: University of California Press, 1975.

Deals with the emigration of peasants from one Chinese village between 1969 and 1971. The author's work focussed on an intensive investigation of the village of San Tin, the largest emigrant community in Hong Kong, and a brief follow-up survey of San Tin emigrants working in London. A central theme throughout the study is the relationship between emigration and social change.

Williams, Lea E. *The Future of the Overseas Chinese in Southeast Asia.* New York: Council on Foreign Relations, 1966. Vol. 4: The U.S. and China in World Affairs.

Study of overseas Chinese in the mid-1960s. Concludes that they have divorced themselves from the politics of Communists vs. Nationalists and are trying to assimilate themselves, especially in Singapore and Malaysia, to lose their "cultural distinctiveness."

Willmott, D., *The Chinese of Semarang: A Changing Minority in Indonesia.* Ithaca, N.Y.: Cornell University Press, 1960.

Willmott, W. E., editor. *Economic Organization in Chinese Society.* Stanford: Stanford University Press, 1972.

A series of 13 papers examining the system of social relationships that underlies and surrounds Chinese economic activity in mainland China, Hong Kong, and Taiwan.

_____. *The Political Structure of the Chinese Community in Cambodia.* New York: Athlone, 1970.

An examination of the Chinese community in Cambodia, including religious, social, economic, and political aspects. Includes a comparison with other overseas Chinese communities.

Wong, John. *ASEAN Economy in Perspective.* Hong Kong: Macmillan, 1979.

A view of the ASEAN economy as a whole. The author looks at trade as an "engine for growth and dependency," industrialization, agricultural and rural development, and the socioeconomic framework of development. He concludes that the open ASEAN economy, combined with various incentives and concessions, has resulted in a very high level of foreign investment. This has led to all of the ASEAN countries experiencing economic growth.

Wong, John, editor. *The Cities of Asia.* Singapore: Singapore University Press, 1976.

A collection of the papers presented at the International Seminar on Urban Land Use Policy, Taxation, and Economic Development held in Singapore. The papers are divided into two parts dealing with managing and financing urban land development.

Wu, David Y. H. *The Chinese in Papua New Guinea: 1880-1980.* Hong Kong: Chinese University Press, 1982.

The author follows the evolution of overseas Chinese from both a historical and an anthropological viewpoint. In analysing the fact that most Chinese are involved in commercial operations, he considers kinship, socio-political organizations and political transitions. Both historical documents and biographical excerpts aid in the analysis. Finally, he concludes with a summary and conjecture about the future of the overseas Chinese in Papua New Guina.

Wu, Yuan-li, and Chun-hsi Wu. *Economic Development in South East Asia: The Chinese Dimension.* Stanford: Hoover Institution, 1980.

Looks at the Chinese and their effect on South East Asian economic development. The authors consider the current South East Asian economy and its growth prospects. An examination of Chinese economic activities and how they are viewed by South East Asians follows. Finally, they view the South East Asian's economic activities with their neighbours and allies. They conclude that the Chinese are major factors to be considered when discussing the economic future of South East Asian nations.

Youngson, A. J. *Hong Kong Economic Growth Policy.* Hong Kong: Oxford University Press, 1982.

The book traces the history of Hong Kong's growth over the last thirty years and examines the circumstances and policies that have fostered it.

Yung, Cheng Tong. *The Economy of Hong Kong.* Kowloon, Hong Kong: Far East Publications, 1982.

A case study description of the Hong Kong economy and its related political, environmental, and sociocultural aspects. In addition to making available the author's own research and analyses, the book attempts to provide the reader with all major findings produced by other research projects.

Zagaris, Bruce. *Foreign Investment in the U.S.* New York: Praeger, 1980.

Compiles information relevant to the foreign investor who is interested in U.S. real estate and/or natural resources. Covers legal and tax matters, the "actors," and the steps to be followed. A more detailed look at specific investments follows: urban property, agricultural property, timber, energy, mineral resources, and non-energy mineral resources.

NEWSPAPERS

"The banking rivals: freedom, laissez-faire put Hong Kong on top." *Financial Times* (Toronto), 25 June 1979, p. 17.

Clarke, John. "Why B.C. land draws investors from abroad." *Globe and Mail*, 13 December 1980, p. 8.

Conrad, Richard. "Report concludes foreign ownership of land is beneficial." *Globe and Mail*, 18 February 1977, p. 83.

Constantineau, Bruce. "B.C. stability draws Asian investment." *The Sun* (Vancouver), 15 July 1983, p. B5.

Cook, Peter. "Southeast Asia." *Financial Times* (Toronto), 25 June 1979, pp. 15-16.

A brief history of ASEAN, its information, goals, and accomplishments.

Daniels, Alan. "Crisis of confidence: Hong Kong money quietly moves West." *The Sun* (Vancouver), 20 May 1983, p. E1.

Drinkhall, Jim, and Janet Guyon. "(U.S.) Real Estate purchased by foreigners climb, stirring wide debate." *Wall Street Journal*, 26 September 1979, p. 1.

Ford, Ashley. "Georgia Hotel doomed to disappear." *The Province* (Vancouver), 24 January 1982, p. 1.

"Foreign investment blamed for driving up land prices." *The Sun* (Vancouver), 14 November 1980, p. 6.

"Foreign investment rises to $46.9 billion." *Globe and Mail*, 9 October 1980, p. B5

"Foreign land bill called too far ranging." *Globe and Mail*, 11 June 1976, p. 82.

"Foreign land buyers a minority." *The Province* (Vancouver), 1 February 1981, p. A6.

Gilbert, Michael. "Developers have taken the road south." *Financial Post*, 9 October 1976, pp. P1-P2.

Political barricades, both provincial and federal, have been the main contributing factors. Far Eastern investors are heading south for the same reasons.

"The Hong Kong connection." *Financial Post*, 19 February 1977, p. 24.

Imlach, Andy. "Bill restricts foreigners buying land in Alberta." Edmonton Journal, 22 April 1977, p. 1.

"The land grabs." *The Province* (Vancouver), 5 December 1980, p. B1.

B.C. must consider implementing control over foreign ownership. No restrictions, plus a depressed Canadian dollar makes the province especially attractive. No restrictions may be creating an unstable market.

Lukasiewicz, Mark. "Singapore is a hub for Asian business." *Globe and Mail*, 17 October 1979, p. B4

"Malaysia has a lot to offer investors." *Financial Post*, 27 September 1980, p. 12.

Malaysian Industrial Development Authority (MIDA) Act. *Financial Times* (Toronto), 25 June 1979, pp. 20-21.

Advertisement to stimulate investment. Among other things, mentions availability of developed land at cheap prices ($US2.20 - 20 PSM), low wages for labour ($US1.35 - $US2.25 per day), tax holidays, and political and economic stability.

Nutt, Rod, and Brian Power. "Asians drawn to Vancouver by real estate." *The Sun* (Vancouver), 22 June 1982, p. C5.

Pritchard, Chris. "Australia learns it belongs to hard world." *The Sun* (Vancouver), 14 September 1982, p. B5.

Ricketts, Mark. "Foreign real estate investors see some faults in the lay of land." *Financial Post*, 23 October 1976, p. 19.

————. "Quebec limits foreign land ownership." *Financial Post*, 9 October 1976, p. B8.

Shiller, Edward. "Study sees need of foreign cash for real estate." Toronto Star, 16 February 1977, p. C9.

Shulman, Michael. "Making Canada more attractive to Hong Kong Investors." *Financial Post*, 17 November, 1984, p.14.

Explores factors that attract Hong Kong capital and observes that presently more needs to be done.

Smith, Lawrence. "Limiting foreign ownership can do more harm than good." *Financial Post*, 9 October 1976, p. P10.

Turnbull, Malcolm. "B. C. shuts crown farmland sales to foreigners." *The Province* (Vancouver), 17 July 1980, p. 1.

Turner, Julia. "Is land going to aliens? Provinces don't know." *Globe and Mail*, 27 July 1979, pp. 1-2.

MISCELLANEOUS (GOVERNMENT REPORTS, UNPUBLISHED REPORTS, ETC.)

GOVERNMENT PUBLICATIONS

Government of Australia, Parliamentary Paper, No. 396. *Foreign Investment in Australia.* Canberra, 1978.

Australian government policy on foreign investment, including procedural process. Investments that are in the best interests of the country and that have some local participation are preferred. To attract investors, a stable investment climate with attractive opportunities must be offered.

United States Government, Department of Agriculture. *Foreign Investment in U.S. Real Estate.* February 1977.

Summary of findings of twenty papers on socio-economic impacts on foreign investment in U.S. land. Concludes that American policy should consider whether citizenship status is conditional for U.S. land ownership and if information on land ownership should be readily available to the public.

SERIALS

New Town (N.T.) Properties Limited. Annual Report 1982. Hong Kong.

Kwok Tak Seng, chairman, notes that the uncertainty of 1997 affects long-term investment, especially in the property market. An abatement in interest rates should help revive the market.

Sun Hung Kai Properties Limited. Annual Report 1982. Hong Kong.

In his chairman's statement, Kwok Tak Seng says that the property market has been affected by worldwide high interest rates and thus a general recession. This has meant that the company has followed a conservative policy for the last year. He forecasts that the market will improve with an improvement in the general economy and a clarification of Hong Kong's future.

UNPUBLISHED MATERIAL

Hamilton, Stan, and David Baxter. "Alien and non-resident land ownership." Report No. 18, U.B.C., *Report and Reprint Series.* Vancouver: U.B.C., 1976.

Discusses alternative controls on alien land ownership, the Ontario Land Transfer Tax, and the effectiveness of controls on alien and non-resident land ownership, using PEI and Ontario as examples.

Hicks, G.L., and S.G. Redding. "Industrial East Asia and the Post-Confucian hypothesis: A Challenge to economics." Hong Kong: Dept. of Management Studies, University of Hong Kong, 1982. (Mimeographed)

This paper documents East Asian economic success and attempts to illustrate the difficulties which social scientists are having in explaining it.

————. "Uncovering the sources of East Asian economic growth." Hong Kong: Dept. of Management Studies, University of Hong Kong, 1983. (Mimeographed)

This paper reviews the work of social scientists who have attempted to describe the influence of culture as part of the explanation for East Asia economic success. The authors conclude that more coordinated work is needed and propose a framework for doing this.

Howard, Jennifer A. "The impact of foreign investment on the Canadian economy." Thesis. Victoria: University of Victoria, 1979.

Looks at the history and trends of foreign investment in Canada with corresponding Canadian policies. Concludes that Canada has been, and will continue to be, too dependent on foreign capital and that policies formed have been slow and ineffective in dealing with foreign investment.

Kwok, R. Yin-Wang. "Communication Needs in Hong Kong's Development." Hong Kong: Centre for Urban Studies and Urban Planning, University of Hong Kong, 1982.

McGee, T.G. "Circuits and networks of capital: The internationalization of the world economy and national urbanization." Vancouver, B.C.: Institute of Asian Research, University of British Columbia, 1984. (Mimeographed)

A paper on contemporary urbanization in developing countries. Suggests future research priorities should include evaluating the movements of capital which fuels the growth of cities. Author feels that understanding these processes will lead to more effective policy formation for the cities of Asia.

Moench, R. U.. "Economic relations of the Chinese in the Society Islands." Ph.D. Thesis, Harvard University, 1963.

Price Waterhouse. *Singapore as an International Finance Centre.* Singapore: Price Waterhouse, 1976.

Study done by Price Waterhouse showing the advantages of investing in Singapore. Details tax implications as well as more detailed information regarding financial operations in Singapore.

Ross, P. S. *Impact of Foreign Investment in Commercial and Multiple Family Residential Real Estate in the Greater Vancouver Area.* Real Estate Board of Greater Vancouver, March 1974.

Looks at the impact of foreign investment on commercial and multiple family residential properties. Concludes that foreign investment is good: it provides more multiple family units than would otherwise be available, increases employment, income and cash flow.

Spencer, John. *The Alien Landowner in Canada.* Vancouver: U.B.C., 1974.

The law and its effect on the alien landowner. Concludes that provinces have no jurisdiction regarding restriction unless the owner is not a resident of the province in which the land is located; however, the provinces may restrict the granting of public land to foreigners.

Thrift, Nigel. "World cities and the world city property market: The case of Southeast Asian investment in Australia." Canberra: Australian National University, Department of Human Geography Research, School of Pacific Studies, 1983.

This paper is concerned with one aspect of world city formation, namely the "world city property market." The paper is divided into four parts: reasons for the formation of world cities; a look at the world city property market; a study of Southeast Asian investment in urban real estate in the Pacific Basin; and an examination of one property company — the Hong Kong Land Company.

PERIODICALS AND WORKING PAPERS

Alexander, Charles P. "Fighting it out." *Time*, 1 August 1983, pp. 36-39.

Japanese competitiveness domestically ensures success abroad. At home, success means exceptionally low prices, outstanding quality, and innovative features.

"A 99-year land grab." *Asiaweek*, 9 June 1978, p. 78.

Apgar, Mahlon, IV. "The Changing Realities of Foreign Investment." *Urban Land*, Vol. 43, No. 11, November 1984, pp. 6-11.

"Asean tycoons in China." *Asiaweek*, 15 August 1980, pp. 40-41.

"Asia's quarter-century." *Asiaweek*, 7 January 1983, pp. 42-43.

"Asian invasion down under." *Asiaweek*, 22 May 1981, pp. 41-42.

"Assessing the stakes." *Asiaweek*, 8 October 1982, pp. 30-31.

Regarding the effects of Hong Kong's future on Taiwan and Southeast Asia. The matter is especially important for Taiwan because if Hong Kong reverts to China, there will be pressure on Taiwan to rejoin China.

Awanohara, Susumu. "We manufacture more new ideas than things." *Far Eastern Economic Review*, 13 August 1982, pp. 46-48.

The article focusses on trade among the ASEAN nations. Since four of them rely on the same export commodities, trade with other Pacific Basin countries (Japan, U.S., Canada, Australia) has been initiated.

_____. "Shortage sends prices soaring in Singapore." *Far Eastern Economic Review*, 16 January 1981, pp. 40-43.

_____. "Bombs in Chinatown: Explosions in Jakarta's commercial centre focus attention on resentment of Chinese and army reaction to recent riots." *Far Eastern Economic Review*, 18 November 1984, pp. 18-19.

Highlights the continuing threat to overseas Chinese in Indonesia.

"Bad week for the fruitful." *Asiaweek*, 3 June 1983, pp. 48-49.

The background behind the fall of the once-mighty Hong Kong dollar. The article concludes that the decline is mainly fuelled by the 1997 question.

"Bank Bumi's Hong Kong loans are now an umno issue." *Far Eastern Economic Review*, 5 May 1983, pp. 90-91.

"Banking on growth." *Asiaweek*, 9 April 1982, p. 31.

Many foreigners are buying up U.S. banks and must therefore meet more stringent information requirements. For example, the Liem family "has substantial interests in Indonesia, Hong Kong, and the Asia-Pacific region, including banking, finance . . . and property.

Barnett, Milton L. "Kinship as a factor affecting Cantonese economic adaptation in the United States." *Human Organization*, Vol. 19, No. 1, pp. 40-46, 1960.

The article examines the interrelationships between kinship and economic orientation for Chinese-Americans in North American urban situations. The findings are that economic adaption has been accompanied by a persistent adherence to much of the Kwangtung social structure and behavioural norms — of which kinship and quasi-kinship relations play an important part.

"The barons step in." *Asiaweek*, 9 October 1981, p. 37.

Bartholomew, James. "Sound base for the bulls." *Far Eastern Economic Review*, 5 September 1980, pp. 85-86.

_____. "Stagnation in one sector." *Far Eastern Economic Review*, 13 February 1981, pp. 53-54.

"Battle of the giants." *Asiaweek*, 4 July 1980, pp. 40-41.

Benzer, Shirley L. "Why foreigners are buying up so much U.S. real estate." *Institutional Investor*, July 1977, pp. 88-91.

"Billion dollar antics." *Asiaweek*, 19 September 1980, p. 42.

Blackburn, Mark. "Investors are at bay on the Bay." *Far Eastern Economic Review*, 24 February 1983, pp. 62-63.

A look at the U.S. West Coast real estate market, with a focus on San Francisco. Concludes that low interest rates make it a buyer's market, but there is not enough of them to exert upward pressure on the price of houses.

Bonavia, David. "One step at a time." *Far Eastern Economic Review*, 6 August 1982, p. 15.

China is still trying to clarify the 1997 expiry of the lease on Hong Kong, while British governor Edward Youde warns that it cannot all be settled at once. Possible solutions are also discussed.

"The boom in property values." *Asiaweek*, 8 September 1978, pp. 34-39.

Views property markets in Hong Kong, Singapore, Malaysia, and Indonesia.

"Booming Malaysia presses for industrialization." *Business Week*, 13 April 1981, pp. 66-73.

Bowring, Philip. "Black mark for a red cadre." *Far Eastern Economic Review*, 9 June 1983, p. 75.

Criticisms made by the Hong Kong head of the Bank of China, Jiang Wengui, about the market system led to a fall in the Hong Kong dollar. His remarks raise the question of whether Peking can really keep out of Hong Kong's administration after 1997.

————. "Catch a falling star." *Far Eastern Economic Review*, 27 January 1983, pp. 60-62.

The salvaging of Carrian appears even more doubtful as more facts about the company come to light. Several transactions may not have been arms-length, and there are some doubtful receivables on the books.

————. "Yesterday's men of property." *Far Eastern Economic Review*, 26 November 1982, pp. 59-60.

Former high rollers are now suffering from the follies of their activities — high interest costs. Disruption has been kept to property and financial sectors.

————. "Carrian's private parts." *Far Eastern Economic Review*, 19 November 1982, pp. 91-93.

There are rescue operations in effect for both Carrian and Eda Investments, staving off the possible collapse of other similar companies. However, secured creditors are unhappy that less prudent, unsecured creditors are getting the same treatment.

————. "A two-legged limp." *Far Eastern Economic Review*, 8 October 1982, pp. 58-59.

A gloomy economic forecast for Hong Kong, which is shaken by 1997 jitters.

————. "Greed begets glut." *Far Eastern Economic Review*, 24 September 1982, pp. 140-141.

A fall in prices in what is needed to bring down the oversupply of buildings in Hong Kong.

_____, and Mary Lee. "Tread softly, Iron Lady." *Far Eastern Economic Review*, 17 September 1982, pp. 23-27.

The success of Margaret Thatcher's visit to Peking will depend largely on her ability to reach an agreeable compromise diplomatically.

_____, and Mary Lee. "Dear friends . . . ." *Far Eastern Economic Review*, 13 August 1982, p. 114.

The Hong Kong sale of a prime office site to the Bank of China at a conciliatory price had exactly the opposite effect of what it was intended to do: bolster shaky investor confidence.

"Breaking free." *Asiaweek*, 18 July 1980, pp. 20-26.

Women in Asian business are "ambitious, highly motivated . . . achieving real success on terms of absolute equality with men," but they first have to break down prejudices that a woman's place is in the home.

Brody, Michael. "Runaway boom: Hong Kong money pours into 'Frisco real estate." *Barron's*, 3 July 1978, p. 9.

Brown, C. M. G. "Singapore's office market — expensive and becoming more so." *Unibeam*, 10, 1981, pp. 130-38.

"The bullion called Singapore land." *Asiaweek*, 30 May 1980, p. 46.

Buruma, Ian. "China uses patriotism to encourage the support of its overseas sons: Call of the motherland." *Far Eastern Economic Review*, 22 November 1984, pp. 46-51.

"Buying the competition." *Asiaweek*, 8 April 1983, pp. 65-67.

Hong Kong Land sells 34.8 per cent of Hong Kong Telephone Co. to British Cable and Wireless PLC. Speculation is that Hong Kong's largest property company needs the cash.

"Canada's thrust across the Pacific." *Asiaweek*, 26 September 1980, pp. 44-52.

Positive economic indicators increase Canada's attractiveness as Ottawa tries to attract Asian investors.

"A case of Hong Kong flu." *Asiaweek*, 24 November 1978, p. 56.

There was panic in the stock market because of rising interest rates and some prime real estate that could not be sold for its overoptimistic selling price.

Catino, Jean E. "City review: Oakland/East Bay." *National Real Estate Investor*, January 1982, pp. 5+

Mentions that a $US300 million Asian trade centre, the Trans Pacific Centre, is being built by Asian Holdings, Inc. — a joint venture of three Hong Kong real estate firms. Included in the centre will be office, retail, and residential space and possibly a major hotel. The influx of Hong Kong money is attributed to investor uncertainty about the expiry of the Hong Kong lease from the People's Republic to Britain in twenty years.

"A challenge for the property men." *Asiaweek*, 30 October 1981, pp. 37-38.

The Hong Kong government is revising its Home Ownership Scheme rules, originally designed to make housing more affordable for lower- and middle-income people. Private property developers say that although the new rules will depress property prices, most of the apartments are in the New Towns which have unattractive locations.

"The changing of the guard at Noble House." *Newsweek*, 18 April 1983, pp. 60-61.

David Newbigging is replaced by Simon Keswick as the head of Jardine, Matheson and Company — Hong Kong's largest and most prestigous trading company.

Cheah, Cheng Hye. "Banks are now jumpy about lending anywhere." *Far Eastern Economic Review*, 5 May 1983, pp. 69-70.

Chesser, Thomas. "Club for the clobbered." *Far Eastern Economic Review*, 6 January 1983, pp. 80-81.

A group of Asian businessmen have proposed to form their own EEC: Asia Pacific Economic Community (APEC), to help coordinate trade and economic cooperation between the member countries.

"China: A special relationship." *Asiaweek*, 26 September 1980, p. 61.

Canada shares a close relationship with China.

"The Chinese alternative." *Asiaweek*, 29 February 1980, p. 36.

Cheap housing in the province of Guangdong is viewed as an alternative to high rent Hong Kong.

Chong, Phijit. "Cash before the nail." *Far Eastern Economic Review*, 9 February 1980, p. 79.

The three Hong Kong developers investing in China so far have been doing extremely well, generating a 20 per cent return on investment. The projects are carried out on a joint venture basis, where the Chinese claim 35 per cent of all units built, or on a compensation trade basis, where the developer has to build twice as many units for the Chinese as for himself.

_____. "Room with a view of China." *Far Eastern Economic Review*, 8 February 1980, pp. 79-80.

Large-scale housing units in China being built by Hong Kong developers have proven extremely successful, selling at least one year in advance. The interest is generated mostly by overseas Chinese in Hong Kong and Southeast Asia who cite price, sentimental reasons, location, and an apparently stable political climate as factors for their investments.

_____. "Shenzhen looks to the commuter." *Far Eastern Economic Review*, 15 February 1980, p. 56.

Nearly 3000 people in two days rushed to buy the 216 apartments, thus indicating the demand for Chinese land. The project is to be a supporting scheme in building up local industry. Incentives offered are: duty free imports of electrical appliances for home use, special car licences and multiple re-entry permits for commuters, and telephone installation.

Clad, James. "Umno Challenges the opposition over who is more Islamic, than Whom: They Shall Not PAS." *Far Eastern Economic Review*, 18 October 1984, pp. 16-18.

Discusses continuing political problems in Malaysia resulting from Islamic fundamentalists and their splinter party PAS.

Clad, James. "Vitriol and fisticuffs: The country's most important Chinese political party remains divided in its biggest and most bitter leadership dispute." *Far Eastern Economic Review*, 22 November 1984, pp. 29-30.

"Confidence motions." *Asiaweek*, 20 August 1982, p. 48.

The Bank of China's Hong Kong headquarters purchased at $1HK billion is seen to be a very low price, at two-thirds the going rate. This is doing very little to instill confidence.

"Conspiracy of silence." *Asiaweek*, 3 April 1981, pp. 26-30.

Britain's proposed Nationality Bill is raising fears in Hong Kong that Britain is abandoning its responsibility to its last major colony. This is in addition to 1997 anxieties.

"The countdown begins." *Asiaweek*, 8 October 1982, pp. 27-31.

During Margaret Thatcher's visit to China, both countries agreed on the importance of maintaining Hong Kong's stability and prosperity. Their differences regarding sovereignty, with each claiming the right, led to a plunging stock market.

"The crack of dawn." *Asiaweek*, 7 May 1982, p. 21.

Hong Kong land has acquired 35 per cent of both the telephone and the electricity company. The reason appears to be the strategically located sub-stations and maintenance depots, over which high-rises could be built.

Cutler, Maurice. "Foreign demand for our land and resources." *Canadian Geographical Journal*, April to July/August 1975.

A series of five articles dealing with the topic of foreign investment. Various studies are cited including those done by P. S. Ross (Vancouver), J. Walter Thompson (Montreal), and the Select Committee on Cultural and Economic Nationalism (Ontario). The fourth article, "How foreign owners shape our cities" is of particular interest as it deals with capital flows in and out of Canadian metropolitan areas.

Daly, Maurice T. "The revolution in international capital markets: urban and Australian cities." *Environment and Planning A*, Vol. 16, pp. 1003-20.

The emergence of Eurodollar and other international capital market innovations are traced out and related to dramatic changes in financing urban development in Australia.

Davenport, Andrew. "Land act qualms in Malaysia." *Far Eastern Economic Review*, 2 January 1976, pp. 42-43.

Criticizes the Malaysian amendment to the Land Acquisition Bill, which Davenport believes will discourage private, especially foreign, investment. The amendment was designed to prevent speculation in real estate acquisition (usually agricultural land) plans by valuing the land based on current output rather than on potential or market value.

Davies, Derek, et. al. "Initialled, sealed and delivered: An unprecedented agreement guarantees the future." *Far Eastern Economic Review*, Vol. 126, No. 40, pp. 12-17, 1984.

This is the *FEGR*'s analysis on the Sino-British accord on Hong Kong.

Davies, Derek, and Mary Lee. "Community begins at the home." *Far Eastern Economic Review*, 10 December 1982, pp. 67-69.

Increasing independence is helping East Asia to grow amid world recession.

————. "Don't panic, chaps." *Far Eastern Economic Review*, 8 October 1982, pp. 8-11.

Ill-chosen remarks from both Britain and China caused a stock market slide. In an attempt to calm the panic, British governor Youde announced that negotiations have begun.

Delfs, Robert. "A lender dwarfing all competitors." *Far Eastern Economic Review*, 5 May 1983, p. 72.

State-owned Bank of China is head and shoulders above their competitors, both local and foreign. An added advantage is that they do not have to suffer from the same strict anti-profit laws that foreign banks are subject to.

————. "Belated boom: China's home-builders try to make up for wasted time but problems remain." *Far Eastern Economic Review*, 30 April 1982, pp. 41-44.

DeMott, John S. "At the end of a floating pipeline." *Time*, 1 August 1983, p. 40. Energy-poor Japan tries to maximize its use of oil.

"Digging up a billion dollars." *Asiaweek*, 25 December 1981-January 1982, pp. 43-44.

The government-funded Mass Transit Railway (MTR) Corp. has begun digging the Island Line, an underground subway. Financing has come from the sale of land above ground to Hang Lung Development and its consortium, who will also design the underground system and the residential and commercial complexes which will be on top.

"A doctor for Carrian." *Asiaweek*, 28 January 1983, pp. 36-42. Australian Bill Wylie is brought in to save the Carrian conglomerate, "one of the biggest, most vigorous, most diversified, and most mysterious corporate entities in Asia," from being liquidated.

Donald, John. "The influence of foreign investors on Canadian real estate." *Canadian Business*, June 1975, pp. 56-62.

Downs, Anthony. "Money and real estate: growing influx of foreign capital will boost prices." *National Real Estate Investor*, January 1977, p. 46.

Foreigners invest because they want to preserve their assets (thus, look for political and legal stability) and/or to avoid monetary instability. Ownership also gives foreigners a reason to emigrate. There are obstacles however, such as legal and tax differences or unscrupulous advisers.

Ellis, Richard. "Australia: general strength seen, but retail area is overbuilt." *National Real Estate Investor*, January 1982, p. 42.

————. "Hong Kong: continued strong demand causing prices to rise." *National Real Estate Investor*, January 1981, p. 50.

————. "Hong Kong: tightening office sector leads to higher rents." *National Real Estate Investor*, January 1982, pp. 42-43.

————. "Singapore: general optimism leads to healthy realty market." *National Real Estate Investor*, 24 January 1982, pp. 43-45.

Elmer-Dewitt, Philip. "Finishing first with the fifth." *Time,* 1 August 1983, p. 55.

The Japanese are striving to be first in the fifth generation computer race: artificial intelligence.

Etzioni, Amitai. "Mixed scanning: A 'third' approach to decision-making." *Public Administration Review,* Vol. 27, No. 3, pp. 385-92, 1967.

Three conceptions of decision-making are considered here with assumptions that give varying weights to the conscious choice of the decision-makers. The three approaches/models of decision-making discussed in the article are: rationalistic, incrementalist, and mixed scanning.

Feder, Jack. "Planning under foreign investment in Real Property Tax Act of 1980." *Taxes,* 59, February 1981, pp. 81-92.

The Real Property Tax Act of 1980 is analysed and evaluated in terms of the U.S. government's goal: to tax gains made from the sale of U.S. real estate. Basically losses/gains from disposition by a foreigner must be reported and hence is subject to the same taxation rules as U.S. taxpayers.

"Foreign interests snap up real estate." *Business Week*, 11 August 1973, p. 52.

Many investors are purchasing Canadian property because of its "rare stability, solid economic growth, lack of exchange controls, and relatively low tax rates." Incentives include a low 15 per cent withholding tax on dividend or interest income (compared to the 25 per cent charged in the U.S.)

"Foreign investment reaching peak due to limited product." *National Real Estate Investor*, April 1981, p. 18.

"Foreign investors spell out their shopping priorities." *National Real Estate Investor*, July 1981, pp. 18-20.

U.S. real estate is preferred because of higher yields, more prime product, and a stable political climate. They search for offices, hotels, and shopping centres — "100 per cent prime real estate" — with an IRR of 15 per cent over ten years. Property management is a big concern as U.S. property managers are less willing to take a long term view.

"Foreign land buying no problem in B. C. minister maintains." *Canadian Real Estate*, March 1981, p. 2.

Jim Chabot, land, parks and housing minister, said after reviewing 1980 citizenship declarations under the Land Titles Act: of 84 per cent personal declarations, only 1.2 per cent were filed by foreigners. He did admit that not all foreign ownership was included though (such as trust arrangements).

Fraser, Ian. "Boom on the West Coast." *Far Eastern Economic Review*, 20 March 1981, pp. 62-64.

Article on the influx of Southeast Asia investment in Vancouver property, particularly in the residential sector. It is claimed that returns are somewhat less than those in other parts of North America or in Hong Kong, but are viewed by investors as a stable investment.

Friedman, Jack. "The truth about foreign investors in U.S. real estate." *Real Estate Review*, Summer 1981, pp. 13-15.

Friedmann, John, and Wolff Goetz. "World city formation: an agenda for research and action." *International Journal of Urban and Regional Research*, Vol. 6, No. 3, pp. 309-44, September 1982.

This paper concerns the spatial articulation of the emerging world system of production and markets through a global network of cities. Specifically, it is about the principal urban regions in this network, dominant in this hierarchy, in which most of the world's active capital is concentrated.

"From rags to riches to rags to riches." *Asiaweek*, 7 August 1981, p. 48.

The comeback of self-made millionaire Cheong Kim Hock, after losing his business that made him wealthy the first time.

"George Tan fights back." *Asiaweek*, 4 February 1983, pp. 32-34.

The efforts of Carrian's chairman to save his heretofore successful company.

"A global banker's best bet." *Asiaweek*, 8 January 1982, pp. 25-30.

Owing to their profit potential, Asian nations are able to obtain credit from foreign banks with ease. The risk of political stability is less than their profit potential.

"Gloom and boom." *Asiaweek*, 14 May 1982, p. 43.

The U.S. company Chemical Bank painted a bright economic picture for the Asia-Pacific nations growth rate: Singapore, Hong Kong at 10 per cent; Malaysia, Indonesia, Taiwan at 7.5 per cent (the only drop, by 1 per cent); Thailand at 6.7 per cent; South Korea at 6.5 per cent; and the Philippines at 5 per cent. Inflation would decrease everywhere.

Gonzaga, Leo. "The rent rise could speed up." *Far Eastern Economic Review*, 24 February 1983, p. 56.

Summary of the Philippine property market. Rents in both the commercial and residential sector are up.

—————— "Free port, cheap housing." *Far Eastern Economic Review*, 12 November 1982, pp. 74-75.

The Philippine government hopes that relaxed entry rules and low-cost facilities will attract manufacturing investment.

—————— "Reaching new heights." *Far Eastern Economic Review*, 13 February 1981, pp. 52-53.

General article on the property situation in Manila. Although residential and commercial land is available on favourable terms, inflation and government intervention has led to a loss of its edge over other Southeast Asian cities. Political action to freeze low-rate rents and to regulate land speculation has caused developers to move out of the metro district. Other factors, such as lack of housing units and office space for foreign companies and stiff lease terms also add to the problem.

Gooding, Wayne. "A trip to somewhere." *Far Eastern Economic Review*, 17 February 1983, pp. 50-51.

Report on Canada's Pierre Trudeau's trip to Asia in an unsuccessful attempt to drum up business.

Harney, Kenneth. "Foreign investment: taking stock in America." *Real Estate Today*, March 1980, pp. 10-16.

"Havens for sale." *Asiaweek*, 28 January 1983, p. 15.

Recent ads have been placed by various countries trying to attract both flight money and skilled people.

"The high-tech sector opens to 100% foreign investment." *Far Eastern Economic Review*, 2 June 1983, p. 70.

South Korea's electronics industry is now one of the leading exporters of the world.

Ho, Kok Cheung. "Private developers in the 1980's." *Unibeam*, 1978/80, pp. 77-80.

A brief summary of the major problems of real estate in Singapore. Some solutions are also suggested: abolishment of open bidding, consolidation of small companies, and expansion of business opportunities.

"Hong Kong bounces back." *Asiaweek*, 1 July 1983, pp. 39-40.

The slight improvement in Hong Kong's currency and stocks is the result of positive signs from Peking and London, especially the CCP's statement that "China's plans for the territory would respect both history and reality."

"Hong Kong: Dawn of a New Era." *Asiaweek*, 5 August 1984, pp. 18-33.

As the Sino-British talks moved toward a conclusion, this article documents the progress of the talks and outlines key issues.

"Hong Kong Lives." *Asiaweek*, 5 October 1984, pp. 22-44.

Reviews the protracted Sino-British talks on Hong Kong, analyses future implications for Hong Kong and sets out in full the Sino-British accord of 26 September 1984.

"Hong Kong: Talking Tough." *Asiaweek*, 6 July 1984, pp. 24-33.

Provides details of Sino-British talks at a critical point. Specifically, it reports on the journey to Peking by a distinguished group of Hong Kong citizens to try to ensure basic protections.

"Hong Kong's thorny debate." *Asiaweek*, 29 February 1980, pp. 35-37.

Rent controls are introduced in an effort to slow down spiralling property prices.

"To Hong Kong via China?" *Asiaweek*, 18 January 1980, p. 41.

An international airport is planned, to be located in China, and is seen as the "first eraser stroke in the 'vanishing border' between (Hong Kong) and China."

Hoon, Shim Jae. "Raiding the land bank." *Far Eastern Economic Review*, 27 February 1981, pp. 82-84.

The South Korean real estate market, with Seoul as its focal point, has joined the ranks of its Southeast Asian peers, as Seoul land prices are the highest in the world, behind Hong Kong and Tokyo. To obtain more land for development, the government has ordered the country's 1100 largest business firms to release some of their idle land holdings.

"A hotel-building boom by foreign investors." *Business Week*, No. 2689, 25 May 1981, p. 78.

Most of the money is from Singapore, with some also from Hong Kong, Malaysia, and Indonesia. Eighteen new hotels are being built, eleven are undergoing major expansions, and there are more than twenty applications for developer permits.

"How fare the hongs of Hong Kong." *Asiaweek*, 16 October 1981, p. 52.

Despite pessimistic economic forecasts, Hong Kong companies are doubling and tripling their profits, higher than ever before. Many claim the situation is the result of "grossly inflated and deliberately manipulated property values" and is thus a false prosperity. Both interest rates and inflation are high, the HK dollar is weak, and the stock market is skaky, all indicative of a depressed economy.

"How much control?" *Asiaweek*, 3 June 1983, pp. 28-29.

The amount of Chinese domination in the Indonesian economy may not be as high as speculated — it is just that the Chinese are in high-profile positions.

"1997: How professionals feel." *Asiaweek*, 8 July 1983, pp. 44-45.

Informal interviews regarding how Hong Kong professionals feel about the territory's future.

Hsu, Michael. "Appeasing nobody." *Far Eastern Economic Review*, 10 June 1972, pp. 39-40.

A criticism of the Hong Kong government's revision of policy regarding renewal of Crown leases: The 20 per cent general cut plus a five-year phasing programme is a weak solution.

"In the doldrums." *Asiaweek*, 8 August 1980, pp. 53-54.

ASEAN governments are getting "involved in construction and deliberately manipulating the industries to achieve desired ends".

"The initiative lies with Peking." *Asiaweek*, 27 October 1978, pp. 36-37.

Interview with Hong Kong Land's Trevor Bedford about a joint venture between his company and two Peking-based companies, located in Tsun Wan.

"Investment and finance." *Asiaweek*, 15 December 1978, pp. 29-58.

Summary of Asian Pacific Rim countries' unprecedented economic growth. The demand for capital resources means an increasing number of international financial institutions.

Jacobs, Jane. "Cities and the wealth of nations." *The Atlantic*, Vol. 253, No. 3, pp. 41-66, March 1984a.

An article on the world economy including the interrelationship between cities as a new theory of economic life.

————. "The dynamic of decline." *The Atlantic, Vol. 253, No. 4, pp. 98-115, 1984b.*

An examination of two ironies of the world economy: the military spending necessary for imperial success assures imperial failure; national programmes to foster development and attack poverty bring about stagnation

"Jakarta opens new areas for investment." *Asiaweek*, 23 June 1978, p. 43.

Jones, Lang, Wootten. "Malaysia: strong economy augers well for industry in 1980." *National Real Estate Investor*, January 1980, p. 86.

————. "Malaysia: demand exceeding supply for CBD office buildings." *National Real Estate Investor*, 24 January 1982, p. 45.

_____. "Singapore: downtown market tightens, retail development on the rise." *National Real Estate Investor*, 22 January 1980, pp. 84-86.

_____. "Sydney: tight real estate market in CBD may lead to rehabilitation projects." *National Real Estate Investor*, January 1980, p. 84.

Kamaluddin, S. "Others falter but Hong Kong building looks all go." *Far Eastern Economic Review*, 103, 30 March 1979, pp. 5456.

Kaye, Lincoln. "A sector much exposed on the downside." *Far Eastern Economic Review*, 5 March 1984, pp. 55-56.

Article dealing with the oversupply of office, retail, residential, and hotel space in Singapore. Author predicts this situation will continue at least through 1987.

Ku, Y. T. "Profit for some." *Far Eastern Economic Review*, 15 August 1963, pp. 507-8.

The Hong Kong government gains approbation through its announced policy on crown leases in which leaseholders have the option of not redeveloping and extending their leases for a premium based on the value of the existing development, or they may redevelop and extend their leases based on the full market value of the land assuming maximum development. The government hopes that this will pro- duce more housing, offices, shops, and factories.

Kurata, Phil. "A home in the motherland." *Far Eastern Economic Review*, 30 January 1981, pp. 53-56.

China is permitting foreign property investment for three reasons: to barter its cheap labour and land for foreign exchange; to attract industrial development, and to give non-mainland Chinese an opportunity to rebuild ancestral links. The Chinese, taking a 70 per cent from each project, stand to earn up to $HK364 million, while the developers usually make a 20 to 30 per cent margin on their investment.

"Laissez-faire." *Asiaweek*, 3 June 1983.

The effect of the Hong Kong government's laissez-faire policy is terrible.

Lee, C. F. "The road to enfranchisement: Chinese and Japanese in British Columbia." *B.C. Studies*, Vol. 30, No. 1, pp. 44-76, 1976.

Lee, Dinah. "Room at the top for a new cock of the walk." *Far Eastern Economic Review*, 5 May 1983, pp. 93-95.

Singapore government-owned Post Office Savings Bank is joining the competitive banking fray. It is sure to have an impact because of its many strategically-located branches and its current tax and legal advantages over other banks.

Lee, Mary. "Softening on hard issues." *Far Eastern Economic Review*, 9 June 1983, pp. 42-44.

Sino-British talks appear to be getting more amicable on the issue of Hong Kong's future after 1997.

_____. "A stake in the future." *Far Eastern Economic Review*, 26 May 1983, pp. 86-87.

Japanese investment in Hong Kong is evidence of their confidence in the future as a financial centre beyond 1997.

————, and Derek Davies. "Hearts ill at ease." *Far Eastern Economic Review*, 17 March 1983, pp. 41-76.

An overview of Hong Kong. Despite Deng Xiaoping's reassurances, people are anxious. They are still tradition-bound in spite of contrary evidence: sophisticated banking and financial community, high technology.

————. "Singapore solicits." *Far Eastern Economic Review*, 17 December 1982, p. 68.

Several countries, including the U.S., Canada, Australia, and the Caribbean, are hoping to attract flight capital from those investors expressing uncertainty about Hong Kong's future. Singapore is unique in that it is seeking technological transfer.

————. "A clearer picture." *Far Eastern Economic Review*, 26 November 1982, p. 24.

Statements made by Chinese leaders give an indication about the future framework of Hong Kong. Recovery of the territory is admitted to be a national policy for the first time.

————. "The point of no return." *Far Eastern Economic Review*, 20 August 1982, pp. 14-15.

A poll by Hong Kong observers indicate that an overwhelming number of residents would prefer Hong Kong to maintain status quo.

————. "A mighty nice gesture." *Far Eastern Economic Review*, 6 August 1982, pp. 48-51.

The Hong Kong government has teamed up with a China-backed consortium in a joint venture to build new towns. It is seen as a bailout of the Mighty City company but the high price paid seems to indicate that the reason for purchasing was more political than economical.

————, and Philip Bowring. "An underground deal: an apparent change in Hong Kong land policy helps the Mass Transit Railway manufacture property profits." *Far Eastern Economic Review*, 26 March 1982, pp. 146-47.

————. "A ceiling on housing." *Far Eastern Economic Review*, 114, 16 October 1981, pp. 106-7.

To provide more lower class housing, the Hong Kong government has legislated that land prices will be excluded from the price of public housing schemes. While this cuts prices approximately in half for the lower income bracket, the middle class still suffers, being caught between the poor and the rich.

————. "Rents hit the roof." *Far Eastern Economic Review*, 29 May 1981, p. 62.
In light of Hong Kong's continuing rent crisis, some factors behind the situation, such as inadequate housing for the poor and middle class, land shortage, high land prices, ineffective government solutions (such as rent controls), and its free property market policy are reviewed. Alternatively, excessive speculation may cause a market collapse.

————. "Macau has its own mini-boom." *Far Eastern Economic Review*, 30 January 1981, pp. 52-53.

Property development is being encouraged as a result of diplomatic relations between Portugal and China. The effect on land prices is unclear, as property is sold through tenders rather than auctions. Much of the building thus far is of hotels, upper-class apartments, and some commercial development.

_____. "Mighty city's heavenly hopes." *Far Eastern Economic Review*, 12 September 1980, pp. 48-50.

China Resources, a mainland-owned corporation, is developing plants for a new town in the New Territories. However, there are a number of political (zoning) and financial constraints to overcome first.

_____. "A new town for Macau." *Far Eastern Economic Review*, 4 April 1980, pp. 41-42.

_____. "Wealthy voices in the doom chorus." *Far Eastern Economic Review*, 15 February 1980, pp. 58-59.

In response to rapidly rising rents, the Hong Kong government has proposed a blanket rent freeze at a 21 per cent maximum over two years, to the outrage of property developers, who in response claim that government inertia in releasing land from development is the main reason for the present rent troubles.

"Let the export drive begin." *Asiaweek*, 7 January 1983, pp. 46-47.

A summary of ASEAN's economic performances and projections for the future. Concludes that the next year will have a positive growth rate, with recovery depending on Western economies.

Lewis, John, and Anthony Rowley. "Japan — land of the rising rent." *Far Eastern Economic Review*, 30 January 1980, pp. 49-52.

_____. "Soaring rents and complex laws." *Far Eastern Economic Review*, 30 January 1981, p. 50.

Lewis, Stephen E. "Domestic institutions dominating investment market; foreign fervor is cooled by rising U.S. dollars." *National Real Estate Investor*, September 1981, pp. 40-42.

There is a huge amount of Far Eastern capital coming in, often in $100 million chunks, from Hong Kong or Singapore. The original source of funds is Japan or China, where one is not supposed to accumulate wealth.

Lim, Simon B. H. "The business of real estate development in Singapore." *Unibeam*, 1979/80, pp. 71-76.

"Looking for commodities." *Asiaweek*, 8 September 1978, pp. 31-33.

Hong Kong property looks like the top commodity.

"The Lull in the land." *Far Eastern Economic Review*, 30 March 1961, p. 627.

Hong Kong land prices seemed to have levelled out after its phenomenal rise. High prices and the associated fear of tying up too much capital have been cited as reasons for reduced investment. Reasons for growth include the influx of capital from overseas Chinese in South East Asia and banks giving advances to land investment.

"Luxury living in Manila Bay." *Far Eastern Economic Review*, 2 January 1976, p. 39.

Reviews the CDCP's (Construction and Development Corporation of the Philippines) project to develop 1600 hectares in Manila Bay in return for ownership of half of the land. The rumoured land price of $10 million is a small part of the total expenditure, as a high standard of commercial buildings are expected to be constructed.

"Malaysia: The politics of religion." *Asiaweek*, 24 August 1984, pp. 22-31.

Outlines the on-going battle between the ruling UMNO party in Malaysia and Islamic fundamentalists. This is a continuing issue.

"Malaysia: rapping the firebrands." *Asiaweek*, 14 September 1984, pp. 23-27.

Details the political struggle between Islamic moderates and fundamentalists in Malaysia and provides background on environment within which overseas Chinese live in Malaysia today.

"Malaysia's red book campaign." *Far Eastern Economic Review*, 10 March 1961, pp. 398-400.

The government plans to spend $M440.67 million for rural development. Land is wanted: there are an estimated quarter of a million outstanding applications for land.

"Malaysia: The Rulers Head off a Clash." *Asiaweek*, 3 November 1984, pp. 11-17.
Heading off Islamic Fundamentalism is a major task facing Malaysia's government.

Manggi, Habir, and Anthony Rowley. "The extended (corporate) family of Liem Sioe Liong." *Far Eastern Economic Review*, 7 April 1983, pp. 51-56.

The man, the group, and their investments.

————. "Buoyant — for a while." *Far Eastern Economic Review*, 24 February 1983, pp. 56-61.

Indonesia's property market is buoyant, fed by oil export earnings. Rents climbed in all market sectors, but oncoming glut of office space may slow this down.

"Manila moves in on the family conglomerate." *Business Week*, 17 May 1982, pp. 51-55.

The Philippine government will have to start restructuring the economy after the near-collapse of the banking system. The government has bought into the hardest-hit banks to avert panic. Depth of restriction is dependent on the amount of support the Prime Minister receives from the president.

"Massive housing project." *Far Eastern Economic Review*, 25 January 1962, pp. 147-151.

The Singapore Housing and Development Board planned in 1960 to build 53,000 housing units over five years at a cost of $M195 million and was proceeding on schedule. Land shortage led to the construction of higher buildings (more than twenty storeys).

"A matter of generations." *Asiaweek*, 5 January 1979, pp. 38-39.

Discusses the generation gap between Indonesian parents and their children.

Mayo, Mohs, and Ross H. Munro. "Into the ranks of the rich." *Time*, 25 January 1982, pp. 5-13.

The article relates "Singapore's Success Story" and Prime Minister Lee Kuan

Yew's role in it. The phenomenal growth rate is noted, and it is suggested that the P.M. will have to continue to change to maintain growth.

McDonald, Hamish. "The cost of freedom: Australian institutions find their new opportunities are not as profitable as they had been hoping." *Far Eastern Economic Review*, 25 October 1984 pp. 90-92.

Outlines the recent relaxation of banking rules in Australia and discusses some of the consequences.

McFadyen, Stuart. "The control of foreign ownership of Canadian real estate." *Canadian Public Policy*, Vol. II, No. 1, pp. 65-77, 1976.

McMahan, John. "Foreign investment in U.S. real estate." *Urban Land*, November 1977, pp. 3-6.

"Mixed returns." *Asiaweek*, 5 March 1982, p. 35.

China is trying to enter the oil-drilling servicing industry, requiring many experts to move into Hong Kong and Singapore. They may take up the slack in the office and luxury apartment markets.

"The money scandal: Chun [South Korean president] 'loses face.'" *Asiaweek*, 4 June 1982, pp. 16-18.

Nakamura, Koji. "Landing profits in Japan." *Far Eastern Economic Review*, 13 May 1974, pp. 43-44.

Land prices in Tokyo have doubled in the last three years, thus making the real estate market a profitable venture. On the other hand, 35 per cent of all households claim "housing difficulties" and are unable to improve their conditions owing to spiralling land prices.

"National prudence comes first." *Asiaweek*, 26 September 1980, p. 59.

Interview with Canada's Senior Trade Commissioner, Douglas Campbell, in Hong Kong. He specifies what Canada is best able to offer Southeast Asia: technological capability, coal, agricultural exports.

"(Malaysia's) New premier tries to shed rascist image." *Business Week*, 7 September 1981, p. 50.

The new prime minister is very pro-Malay and supports the New Economic Policy while trying to reassure local Chinese and businessmen that faster growth would be beneficial to all. He wants foreign investors to proceed at the benefit of the country.

"A new supercity." *Asiaweek*, 22 August 1980, pp. 21-28.

Construction of $US500 million Raffles City has begun. It will house a complex of shops, offices, a convention area, and the world's tallest hotel. Also mentioned is the $US350 million project, Marina Centre.

"Are the new towns working?" *Asiaweek*, 11 December 1981, pp. 18-19.

Seven "New Towns" are being built to accommodate the burgeoning population of the New Territories. Thus far they have met with little success: transportation is terrible; housing is ugly and impersonal; and social amenities are sadly lacking. Only provision of jobs has been keeping pace.

Nihill, Julian. "New reporting requirements affect foreign investment in U.S. real estate." *International Tax Journal*, April 1979, pp. 313-25.

"North American foreign markets: two different worlds." *National Real Estate Investor*, April 1980, pp. 18-20.

Describes the basic differences between domestic and foreign investors as well as the principal barriers faced.

"Now, a Hong Kong-Canton highway." *Asiaweek*, 1 February 1980, p. 41.

A joint venture between Hong Kong and Peking to build a 93-acre economic zone. This is seen as a positive indicator of the erasure of the border.

"Now, on with the talks." *Asiaweek*, 24 June 1983, pp. 68-71.

There is a possibility of a break in the stalemate over Hong Kong's future but Peking's strategy may change, owing to the death of its 1997 spokesman, Liao Chenghzi.

Omohundro, John T., "Chinese merchant society in the Philippines." *Philippine Sociology Review*, Vol. 21, 1973, pp. 169-80.

Ong, Seow Beng. "A study of residential land values in Singapore." *Unibeam*, 1980/81, pp. 123-30.

Using regression analysis, the author examines the factors which influence varying land values. He concludes environmental quality and accessibility to the CBD and shopping are important while site size is not.

"The overseas Chinese: a dismal view." *Asiaweek*, 4 February 1983, p. 35.

"A pause for breath." *Asiaweek*, 5 March 1982, pp. 36-39.

The Philippine property market has been stabilizing after a steep fall in 1978 with ensuing recovery in 1981. In Manila, there are plans for a pedestrian shopping mall; in Kuala Lumpur, price of prime space has doubled in the last year and a half; in Singapore, the market is very strong; and in Hong Kong, there is extreme oversupply. Generally, the real estate boom of the last year appears to be levelling off.

"Peking reaches out." *Asiaweek*, 27 October 1978, pp. 34-45.

Peking is increasing its external contact in economic activities, especially with Hong Kong.

Peyman, Hugh. "Malaysia's new concrete jungle." *Far Eastern Economic Review*, 13 February 1981, pp. 51-52.

"Property review." *Far Eastern Economic Review*, 24 February 1983, pp. 42-62.

The Asian property market has been gloomy for the last year owing to worldwide recession and high interest rates. As a result, speculative fever died, property values and rents plunged downwards, and developers yields fell to below their financing costs. The net effect is a supply glut. The bright spots are South Korea and Thailand. The outlook is just as dim for favoured investment areas such as B.C., Australia, U.S. West Coast.

"Reaching for the sky." *Asiaweek*, 21 May 1982, pp. 36-38.

Singapore and Hong Kong are expected to have the world's fastest-growing economies in 1982. Both are experiencing building booms. Malaysia is also doing well, but Thailand and the Philippines are not faring as well.

"Realtors see foreign investment accelerating." *Industrial Development*, November/ December 1976, pp. 30-31.

National Association of Realtors Convention say that as of December 1974, 4.9 million acres of U.S. real estate was owned by foreigners. In California, oriental investment stood at 15 per cent.

"Refusing to roll over and play dead." *Far Eastern Economic Review*, 2 June 1983, p. 77.

About South Korea's textile industry, the mainstay of the economy.

"Rents and rages." *Asiaweek*, 24 July 1981, p. 37.

The Hong Kong government has relaxed rent controls on new and luxury apartments, its first phase of getting rid of rent controls completely. Foreign companies say that may deter them from investing in Hong Kong; others are afraid that developers will ignore the much-needed middle-income housing.

"Restructuring to cope with high costs." *Business Week*, 9 November 1981, pp. 136-38.

South East Asian nations are trying (successfully) to restructure their economies to cope with higher energy prices and more expensive external financing. Hong Kong, Indonesia, Taiwan, and Malaysia will either maintain or continue their growth while both Singapore and the Philippines will suffer.

Richardson, Ron. "First signs of a thaw." *Far Eastern Economic Review*, 24 February 1983, pp. 52-53.

A severely depressed B.C. economy is coming out of the doldrums which saw declining prices, projects being postponed, and some major developers becoming insolvent.

Ricks, David A., and Donald L. Racster. "Restrictions on foreign ownership of U.S. real estate." *Real Estate Review*, Spring 1980, pp. 111-15.

Roberts, William J. "Thailand — Land of smiles and opportunity." *Canada Commerce*, February 1981, p. 3.

An article citing the advantages of investing in Thailand such as government-offered incentives through tax breaks and restrictions from land-ownership.

Robins, Brian. "Sweethearts on parade." *Far Eastern Economic Review*, 24 February 1983, pp. 54-56.

A severe economic recession in Australia has put a halt to the runaway property market, which is not projected to improve greatly, despite "sweetheart deals" to try and stimulate demand.

"Room for recovery." *Far Eastern Economic Review*, 24 February 1983, pp. 61-62.

Malaysia's property market: a slight improvement in the coming year, as long as commodity prices firm up.

Rosenfeld, Seth. "The secret conduit." *Far Eastern Economic Review*, 9 June 1983, pp. 80-81.

California bankers notice a definite influx of Hong Kong Chinese money since Margaret Thatcher's September visit to Peking and Hong Kong.

Rowley, Anthony. "Hanging together rather than hanging separately." *Far Eastern Economic Review*, 5 May 1983, pp. 67-69.

Banks have been hard hit by the combination of a sagging property market and ailing manufacturing industry, both due to recession and high interest rates.

_____. "Imperial designs of the overseas Chinese." *Far Eastern Economic Review*, 14 April 1983, p. 75.

Overseas Chinese are creating financial empires. For example, Liem Sioe Liong's group and the Kweks from Singapore.

_____. "Birth of a multinational." *Far Eastern Economic Review*, 7 April 1983, pp. 44-51.

Indonesian Chinese entrepreneur Liem Sioe Liong has been making many acquisitions. His group of investors are the "first of Asean's Overseas Chinese entrepreneurs to acquire an international corporate identity... (to) attract international investment."

_____. "The rise and rise of Asia's rents." *Far Eastern Economic Review*, 16 January 1981, pp. 36-37.

Asian rents are shown to be among the highest in the world, second only to London. However, there are great speculative gains to be made in Asia, as leases are only two to three years whereas in London, they are typically long leases (25 years). High residential rents are a crucial factor in the Asian situation, as is the fact that Hong Kong, and particularly Southeast Asian Chinese, obtain land as a security element when living in countries with non-Chinese ethnic majorities.

_____. "The supermarket is ready to open." *Far Eastern Economic Review*, 1 November 1984, pp. 56-68.

Details the opening of Japan to foreign banking and previews the looming ascendancy of Tokyo as one of the most important financial centres behind New York, London, and Hong Kong.

"Running scared? Who us?" *Asiaweek*, 17 December 1982, pp. 37-38.

Hong Kong's neighbouring countries (Philippines, Bangkok, Taiwan and Singapore) make preparations for expected flight capital, although there are not yet any signs to support this.

Russell, George. "A new good neighbour policy." *Time*, 1 August 1983, pp. 31-32.

Japan is using trade and aid to expunge old memories of its neighbours.

Sacerdoti, Guy. "Jakarta's jumbled land sector." *Far Eastern Economic Review*, 13 February 1981, pp. 54-56.

Unlike Southeast Asian cities where rent is determined by land value, rent in Jakarta is based instead on the scarcity of buildings and their quality. There is a glut of available land but technological, financial, and political difficulties (for example, foreigners cannot own land in Indonesia) make development a slow and expensive process.

"Scions of privilege." *Asiaweek*, 19 December 1980, pp. 30-34.

Rising young executives who come from wealthy families established by their grandfathers are being sent to prestigious business schools to acquire the skills necessary to keep the family dynasty going.

Segal, Jeffrey. "The squeeze is on." *Far Eastern Economic Review*, 6 August 1982, pp. 44-45.

The recession is getting worse in Malaysia and is not expected to improve until late 1983 at the earliest. Its vital plantations are expected to take an even longer time to recover.

"The sharing experience." *Asiaweek*, 30 April 1982, pp. 34-35.

The article relates the extremely successful Hong Kong opening of an office-sharing complex, the Business Executive Centre, the first in Southeast Asia. Plans are underway for more BEC's.

Sharon, Andre, and Jerrold Mitchell. "South East Asia connection." *Financial World*, 1-15 July 1980, pp. 74-75.

Recommends the Singapore/Malaysia area for investment, citing advantages. For example, Singapore is an international financial centre, and Malaysia is resource-rich.

"Sharpening a vision." *Asiaweek*, 11 June 1982, pp. 53-54.

Overview of Philippine business and investment climate.

Shim, Jae Hoon. "The boom soars higher." *Far Eastern Economic Review*, 24 February 1983, pp. 46-47.

The South Korean property market is one of the few bright spots in Asia, owing to the upcoming Asian and Olympic Games.

Simon, Herbert A. "A behavioral model of rational choice." *Quarterly Journal of Economics*, 69(1)1955:99-118.

This paper attempts to include explicitly some of the properties of the choosing organism as elements in defining what is meant by rational behaviour in specific situations and in selecting a rational behaviour in terms of such a definition.

"Simon says." *Asiaweek*, 15 April 1983, pp. 32-33.

Simon Keswick replaces David Newbigging as senior managing director of Jardine, Matheson and Company. Newbigging remains chairman.

"Simon says it again, louder." *Asiaweek*, 24 June 1983, pp. 59-60.

Simon Keswick takes over as chairman of Jardine, Matheson and Company, replacing David Newbigging.

"Singapore surge." *Asiaweek*, 3 April 1981, p. 34.

Since residential property prices are soaring, the government proposes a ban on resale to curb speculation.

Skinner, G. William. "Change and persistence in Chinese culture overseas: A Comparison of Thailand and Java." *Journal of the South Seas Society*, Vol. 16, 1960:86-100.

This is the classic analysis of the Chinese in Thailand. The Thai-Chinese in contrast to those in Java have become increasingly assimilated and Thai in character.

Smith, Patrick. "In pedestrian precincts." *Far Eastern Economic Review*, 24 February 1983, pp. 50-52.

The slack Singapore property market, dropping prices, and rents are all resulting in increasing competitiveness. This is likely to continue for several years.

_____. "Wary and watchful." *Far Eastern Economic Review*, 12 November 1982, p. 74.

Singapore is being cautious, not yet trying to encourage Hong Kong capital or businessmen.

_____. "Down from the heights: Singapore's economy begins to descend from the heady growth rates of recent years as recession bites." *Far Eastern Economic Review*, 21 May 1982, pp. 62-64.

Looks at Singapore's ability to handle a recession: perhaps the best of all the ASEAN nations. The question is how much of the shock can be absorbed by the domestic sector of an economy that relies heavily on foreign trade and investment. Economic performance is the worst it's been since 1978.

"Soft pedalling a massive surplus." *Far Eastern Economic Review*, 1 October 1982, pp. 47-49.

China has its largest trade surplus ever during worldwide recession.

"The SEZ revolution." *Asiaweek*, 6 August 1982, pp. 22-32.

China's Special Economic Zones (SEZs) are an attempt to begin modernization of the country and improving the economy. More areas have been set aside in the provinces of Guangdong and Fujian, where foreign investment is encouraged, bringing with them modern technology.

"Spectre of 1997," *Asiaweek*, 24 September 1982, pp. 22-36.

The meeting of the heads of Britain and China comes not a moment too soon, given the jitters exhibited recently.

"Spotlight." *Asiaweek*, 20 May 1977, pp. 20-23.

Japan's twenty richest people: there are fewer landowners this year, reflecting the general slump in the real estate market.

Sricharatchanya, Paisal. "High-rise allure." *Far Eastern Economic Review*, 24 February 1983, pp. 52-53.

After a slow start, condominiums in Thailand are exhibiting success. It is the single active sector in an otherwise depressed property market.

_____. "Gearing up for the flight." *Far Eastern Economic Review*, 12 November 1982, p. 71.

Thailand is trying to attract money from jittery Hong Kong investors.

"A struggle for identity." *Asiaweek*, 3 June 1983, pp. 26-37.

Indonesian Chinese have long been subject to anti-Chinese sentiment. The government wants them to assimilate, but its policies differentiate them. The Chinese themselves, especially those born in Indonesia, feel assimilated but are not treated as such by the pribumi (indigenes).

Tanzer, Andrew. "Offshore banking later this year." *Far Eastern Economic Review*, 5 May 1983, pp. 74-76.

Foreign banks have improved access to local funding via easing of government regulations. This could be attributed to economic downturn, easy liquidity, and the challenges facing foreign bankers.

_____. "Waiting in the wings." *Far Eastern Economic Review*, 12 November 1982, pp. 71-74.

Taiwan is poised to take advantage of uncertainty over Hong Kong to increase investment and skilled labour.

_____. "End of a Taipei rents bargain." *Far Eastern Economic Review*, 27 February 1981, pp. 79-81.

"Tapping the National Kitty." *Asiaweek*, 28 November 1980, p. 43.

Singapore government's participation in housing is the Central Provident Fund. It is a compulsory savings scheme which makes money available to low and middle income workers to buy government apartments.

Tasker, Rodney. "Musyawarah gets the key of the door." *Far Eastern Economic Review*, 13 August 1982, pp. 39-42.

_____. "The roots of the problem." *Far Eastern Economic Review*, 5 May 1983, pp. 21-27.

Celebrates the 15th anniversary of ASEAN.

"Terminal fever." *Asiaweek*, 28 November 1980, p. 42.

"Hong Kong's hyper-active property moguls (are) . . . casting acquisitive eyes on . . . transport companies with priceless portfolios of land...in booming, overcrowded Hong Kong, land is the most precious of all commodities, and the right to develop it a sure guarantee of multi-million dollar profits."

"They ask, 'When Will I Be Moved'?" *Asiaweek*, 22 August 1980, pp. 28-29.

Interview with Singapore's Minister for National Development, Teh Cheang Wan, about its housing programme.

"Tourists start a building boom." *Far Eastern Economic Review*, 12 January 1979, p. 72.

A building boom of stores and hotels has started owing to the tourist trade. Accordingly, land prices have also risen greatly. Macau seems to be catching on as a retirement spot for senior Hong Kong residents. Finally, mainland China seems to be interested in joint commercial complexes and developing light industry.

"How trade zones are luring foreign investors." *Business Week*, 11 January 1982, pp. 50-51.

New provincial laws give foreign investors unprecedented rights in China's special southern trade zones: they may sign long-term land leases, set wages, and fire workers. Investors are mainly Chinese from Hong Kong, Macau, and Southeast Asia.

Turner, Michael. "The Hong Kong and Shanghai Banking Corporation." (Chairman's statement for the year 1960). *Far Eastern Economic Review*, 9 March 1961, p. 412.

A great rise in local share and land values was noted, brought on by overseas funds seeking investment. A conservative attitude was proposed as an answer to the land speculation which may push prices too high.

Turner, Stewart. "Hard nose the highway." *Asiaweek*, 24 February 1978, p. 45.
About Hong Kong tax havens.

"The underground connection." *Asiaweek*, 29 May 1981, pp. 36-37.

A recently completed building is being torn down so that a larger one may take its place. The building is more valuable as it is located at the end of the new underground railway.

"A variety of rules and financial systems." *Asiaweek*, 15 December 1978, pp. 33-39.

Describes the commercial banking climate in Hong Kong, Singapore, The Philippines, Thailand, Malaysia, and Indonesia.

"1997: The view from Taiwan." *Asiaweek*, 5 November 1982, p. 17.

Vine, P. A. L. "Hong Kong makes a nonsense." *Far Eastern Economic Review*, 1 April 1972, pp. 129-30.

Takes a look at the Hong Kong government's lease policy, which offers two basic alternatives: to redevelop a lot, in which case the full market value will be charged to renew the 99-year lease; or to keep the lot undeveloped and to be charged a lower rent.

"What ails Hong Kong's dollar." *Asiaweek*, 10 June 1983, pp. 38-43.

Bank of China's unprecedented admittal that it is hurting from the falling dollar, blaming speculation in the foreign currency market, is resulting in heightened anxiety over Hong Kong's future.

Whatmore, Richard. "Hong Kong's land problems." *Far Eastern Economic Review*, 10 May 1962, pp. 275-77.

Suggests that industrial growth is hampered by land policies and the lack of new developable land (owing to bureaucratic delay, fear of oversupply, and the government's laissez-faire attitude towards industrial growth). The solution may lie in getting as much industrial land on the market as soon as possible; otherwise investment may drift to other countries.

————. "Land in Hong Kong." *Far Eastern Economic Review*, 5 July 1962, pp. 29-32.

Discusses the growing pressure on land for residential purposes and the consequent rent increases in Hong Kong; suggests that the government should make money and land available to private investors to subsidize the construction of middle-income housing.

White, John R. "How foreign money buys U.S. real estate." *Appraisal Journal*, January 1979, pp. 59-64.

Expresses view that foreign investors have had a positive influence on the real estate market: American investors have learned to "respect inflation, stress location, look beyond the near term, and never to compromise quality."

"Will runaway rents force companies out?" *Business Week*, 6 July 1981, p. 38.

Increasing housing costs may force many foreign-owned companies to recall their executives. As a result, many companies are moving to lower-cost areas like Singapore and Manila. Others are training local Chinese to take over American-held jobs.

Wilson, Paul. "Advance to go: collect a lot." *Far Eastern Economic Review*, 25 January 1980, pp. 64-65.

Reviews the property market in Hong Kong's central financial district, where prices are comparable to or higher than any other district in the world. Other than the government, the major holder is Hong Kong Land. Important capital sources are equity financing and government-subsidized payments on Crown-auctioned land.

————. "Expensive bridgehead for China traders." *Far Eastern Economic Review*, 16 January 1981, pp. 36-40.

A look at the number of reasons behind the inflated Hong Kong real estate market such as: geography, population, economic attraction, low building costs, etc. Generally, the market seems to be bullish although the extreme high prices and the slowdown in China's modernization programme are signs of worry. The government is maintaining its non-interventionist stance, hoping the market will take care of itself.

Wood, Christopher. "Picking up the pieces." *Far Eastern Economic Review*, 24 February 1983, pp. 48-50.

The sad state of the Hong Kong property market is exacerbated by mounting political uncertainty and massive oversupply.

————. "Maturity matters." *Far Eastern Economic Review*, 10 February 1983, pp. 84-85.

Hong Kong Land takes on a $HK4 billion loan to refinance its short term debt, effectively making all their debt medium- or long-term.

————. "Boom, bust — and fallout." *Far Eastern Economic Review*, 5 November 1982, pp. 90-93.

Rescue operations for Carrian and Eda Investments, two large property companies, have people wondering which other companies will follow.

Wu, Michael. "Housing and land policy." *Far Eastern Economic Review*, 29 August 1963, pp. 615-617.

Gives a general history of the Hong Kong land market and government policy and its effects. Suggests that government profits from crown land may be excessive; therefore, the solution would make more developable land available.

Wu, Yuan-Li. "Chinese entrepreneurs in Southeast Asia." *American Economic Review*, Vol. 73, No. 2, 1983: pp. 112-17.

Yao, Raymond. "Wanted: more open space." *Far Eastern Economic Review*, 18 March 1977, pp. 60-62.

Owing to the growing pressures on Hong Kong land, the government has been making efforts to open up the New Territories. Five large-scale town plans plus a land exchange program are in the works.

"Year end synopsis." *Asiaweek*, 29 December 1978-5 January 1979, p. 25.

ASEAN, South Korea, Taiwan, and Hong Kong continued their impressive economic performances.

"1983: Year of the managers." *Asiaweek*, 7 January 1983, pp. 48-50.

The economic forecast for Asia for 1983: maintenance, if not growth, as long as there is good management.

"Year's ahead." *Asiaweek*, 13 August 1982, p. 40.

The government makes a deal with overextended mighty city: the purchase of land near the China-Hong Kong border.

Yuseco, Francis, Jr. "Debt vs. capacity in Southeast Asia." *Asiaweek*, 15 December 1978, pp. 30-33.

Despite maintaining fairly high debt/equity ratios, the Southeast Asian nations have retained their credit rating. Institutional links have also become more stable.

Author Index

Subject Index